C000128812

Chapter 1

The Plan

After a short but eventful career in Her Majesty's Armed Forces I left with a handful of qualifications, most of which would soon show themselves to be quite useless in civilian life. For example, my explosive qualification. However, the Army did give me several useful skills ranging from, communication skills, discipline, to a driving licence. But above all the Army gave me the BUG that's right, the travel bug. After bouncing around from one job to the other I found myself working in the same factory my dad was working in, my dad worked here after devoting 12 years to the British Armed Forces.

My Mum and Dad moved to a little village near the Yorkshire dales to raise me and my brother in a small farming community. They worked very hard, taking on jobs wherever they could, in factories and private cleaning jobs just to get by and put food on the table.

They have my upmost love and respect for doing this, and many more things besides, but I was 22 years of age and I had just got out of the army, after joining up as a junior soldier at the age of 15 years and 8 months, the youngest age allowed back in 1989. I had no ties, yet I began to feel like my life was all mapped out.

I concluded quite quickly that this was not my idea of LIFE.I was never destined to work in a factory for the rest of my days. I respect that some people want to have a steady job and retire at sixty-five or seventy years of age, but I want to travel the world, meet different people and earn money while I travelled. I would go so far to say that about fifty per cent of people want these things.

Like everything in life you've got to go for it!

It took me two years of thinking about it, talking about it, preparing for it, then finally, the step to no return! I handed in my notice at the factory. Most of my work colleagues were content with their twenty days holiday entitlement per year, to give them this brief window of opportunity to explore new places and cultures. But instead, 9 out of 10 workers decided to go for the soul-destroying package holiday. I'm not knocking these people, if that's what makes them happy so be it, good luck to them all.

But me, on the other hand, had to enjoy my work! I wanted to live my life, meet new people, see new places and experience just a little of what the world had to offer. Most of my workmates said they would do it (but). They all made excuses like 'if I were your age' or 'I have to stay because of my girlfriend'. Anybody can go if they really want to, some people might disagree but whose life is it anyway? Most people were simply just too scared of looking passed their own front door.

So overall my plan was to save a bit of money and hitchhike around Europe and try to find work to fund my travels further. 'Quite a simple plan!' well that's what I thought. My best friend Paul who I went to school with, could see where I was coming from, as his mother travelled extensively when he was younger and had now settled in Germany. According to Paul, she had no regrets for doing her own thing. Paul was going out to visit his mother over Christmas and the New Year, so we planned to meet up for a pint if I was about that way.

In my mind if you really want to do something it's better to have tried, than to always think "What if"? People put their dreams and aspirations on hold for so many reasons, mostly to save other people's feelings.

Even though this is quite honourable and selfless It doesn't mean it's the right thing to do. There's a whole world out there and all I wanted was a look. No harm in that.

From starting to prepare for my trip in December 1992 to going in November 1994, I had thought about everything and planned for most things.

If needs be I had some friends in Germany who I could rely on for help. So, I bought myself some camping equipment, dusted off an old rucksack I found in my Mum and Dads loft. This rucksack resembled an old North Pole explorers backpack, complete with its own bulky external metal frame. It didn't look too comfortable, but it did have some positive points. The main point had to be that it was free! Well, I wasn't the best paid factory worker. At least I could tie my tent, rolling mat and sleeping bag to the frame. Leaving me more room in the main backpack for essentials, such as my personal protection equipment.

Of which consisted of 1 set of hard wood nun-chucks and a six-inch survival knife, complete with its own compass handle, which concealed a sewing kit, a hand line fishing kit, a wire saw, waterproof matches and the knife also came with a handy ankle strap sheath for easy access.

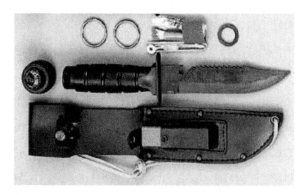

I even had a book with me called The SAS guide to survival.

You may think this was over doing it a bit, other than it was a very informative book. I didn't want to become a casualty, I wanted to be prepared for any and every eventuality!

A week before I was to set off on my travels, I received a call from a friend, asking me if I would be interested in a rail ticket his brother had bought. After a little bit of explaining it became apparent that he had bought a one-month European rail ticket, so he could travel to some football matches across Europe! But his plans went wrong, and he couldn't go anymore. This ticket was valid in over twelve countries and was non-refundable! So, at the resale price of a mere £40, I jumped at this chance to give me a good head start. The ticket wasn't valid to be used in the UK, so there was no change to my plans to hitchhike the three hundred miles to the Dover ferry port and then across to Calais,France.

Chapter 2

The first foot forward

After saying my goodbyes, on a cold misty morning, in late November 1994, I set off on my new adventure. With my rucksack on my back and my thumb pointing skyward I headed of towards Leeds and then the south bound motorway to Dover.

I expected this part of the journey to take no longer than twelve or thirteen hours all I needed was a bit of luck!

I wasn't getting anywhere fast, but my spirits were high, and I wasn't in a race. It was at my pace and not a drill Sergeant's! So, I settled down to a comfortable walking speed and waited for my first lift to come. It was rush-hour everyone was on their way to work.

There must have been an average of thirty cars passing me per minute but that's the point, they were all passing me. I thought to myself after rush hour had passed there would be a better chance of a lift.

I tried to put myself in the commuter's mind. They all needed to get somewhere within a certain time frame, yet I wasn't on a time frame! I convinced myself that I would probably not get picked up while it was this busy. I guess that's why they call it the rat race!

I settled down in my own little dream world, taking in the views of Yorkshire, what I was soon to be far away from. I wondered if there was anywhere out there which would give me the same warm feeling inside as the Yorkshire dales did at that time and still does today.

Germany was renowned for its bad winters, meaning −20oC freezing. I was not about to become a casualty. After walking about five miles I began to realise a big error of judgement on my behalf.

I had everything, the only thing I didn't have was a donkey to carry it all and five miles felt like twenty! I found a sign which said 'Sheffield 20m' at this moment I had been travelling for half a day, I thought I was doing quite well then, I turned to see a sign which read 'Leeds 15m'. After the rush hour it became dead quiet. It was like everyone was playing hide and seek and I was on. The contrast was breath taking! Then out of the silence I could hear an echoing of an engine coming from the distance.

The sound seemed to be coming from all directions, bouncing off the valley walls. Then a sudden silence, I guess this traveller had reached his destination. Leaving me in still quiet once more.
I must have walked fifteen miles or so, with a steady flow of traffic, but still no cars had stopped.

The weather had started to close in. I knew from my teenage years when me and my friends raced the rain on our motorbikes, across the open expanse of the Yorkshire moors, of how quick the weather could change. Then the rain came.

Within a minute of it starting to drizzle it became a full-on down pour. I took shelter under a nearby row of pine trees.

While I stood there, I stretched my opened hand out from the protection of these mighty evergreens, to see one single rain drop hitting the centre of my hand, with a slight sting it exploded on impact, like a hand grenade going off in slow motion! Drenching my hand as the mist settled.

I quickly concluded to make camp in a nearby field, so I could cook up some food and sit out of the rain. I had bought an army twenty-four-hour ration pack just for such occasion. I was hoping to be at least in France before starting to use it though. A tin of chicken curry, a cup of coffee and some fruit biscuits later, I was sat staring out into the rain across a West Yorkshire field.

The light was fading, and it became apparent that the rain was set for the night, so I made myself comfortable for my first night under canvas to restart my journey the next morning.

As the morning sun was rising with the dew glistening on the ground around me, with droplets tracking down the guide ropes like sparkling diamonds I started to gather my things. I didn't get much sleep that night, I must have been camped under a flight path of one of the local airports. Every fifteen minutes an aircraft would go overhead. After shaking the excess water off my tent, I packed it slightly damp then gathered up the rest of my things and made my way back to the roadside to catch the early morning traffic.

To my disbelief after walking with my thumb out for a good five hours, a car pulled in about twenty meters in front of me and put on its hazard lights.

The passenger lent out of his window and shouted, "come on do you want a lift?" with that I ran towards this small blue car with a smile on my face and a warm feeling of Jubilation came over me, as I had my first lift. As I got closer, I could see this man waving me faster, I must have been less than two meters away from the car I could smell the exhaust fumes then all I could hear was the rev of the car's engine and the squeal of the wheels as it pulled away. Within one second my emotions went from cloud nine to rock bottom as I heard laughing coming from the car which disappeared into the distance.

With that I collapsed by the roadside, I sat on my bag in shear disbelief of what had just happened. After a while I pitied this poor excuse for a human being. But none of this could change the fact that the rain was back, and I was exhausted.

It was to be another night under the stars for me! So, I got myself together and made my way down an embankment at the edge of the dual carriageway, I clambered over a dry-stone wall and set up camp in the neighbouring field.

After dragging myself in to my tent just in time for the down poor to start I laid back with my backpack as a pillow and listened to the rain hitting my tent it sounded like a thousand people walking on bubble wrap. I could see and hear each drop bouncing off the canvas as the sound reverberated around me. There was to be no sleep in this rainstorm.

It must have been close to midnight when the rain eventually subsided and with that came a peaceful silence. It felt like the world had stopped spinning and everything had frozen in time. The only sound I could hear was my own heart beating! With a sigh of relief and a brief feeling of loneliness I drifted off to sleep.

After another disturbed night's sleep, I set off hitch hiking at about seven o'clock and by midday I decided I wasn't walking any further. I threw myself to the floor and sat on my backpack by the side of the road. With my feet hanging into the gutter, but I still had my thumb stretched out to the elements still hoping for that illusive lift.

As I sat there with the spray from the passing cars enveloping my face in a fine mist, all I could think about was the people at home who said this trip was foolish. I would be lying if I said I didn't think of giving up, and just going home. I must have been no more than thirty miles from home. Although it would be easy in some ways to go home, in other ways it would have been the hardest decision I would have to make. I didn't want to prove myself wrong and these people back home right, after only three days.

With my head down and my thumb barely raised I was contemplating what I was to do next. As a car past in front of me quite slowly, I glanced over my left shoulder looking towards this passing car to be faced with the glow of red break lights.

It was like I could feel the warmth of the bulbs heating my soul. I began to think, 'Could this be my first lift?' I half expected the car to pull away again if I stood up, but a loud voice called me over, so I dragged myself to my feet and made my way to this small red car.

When I pulled open the front passenger door I was faced with a small middle-aged, red-faced man sitting at the wheel, with a beaming smile on his face.

He asked, "where are you going lad?" I replied "South, just anywhere south mate". "Will Swindon do?" the jovial man asked. "If it's closer to Dover than here, it will do just fine" I replied.

With a feeling of relief, I placed my backpack behind my seat then I got myself comfortable for the next part of my journey. While I was warming my hands on the constant stream of warm air coming from the dashboard. My friendly, temporary travelling companion asked me one simple innocent question, "Were you waiting long for a lift then?" a smile came across my face as I went on to tell this friendly traveller my ordeal so far. After a few minutes of questions and answers, I found out that this man was called Anthony. He was on his way back to work, to join his circus troop just outside Swindon. Anthony was a clown from the circus, which went quite some way to explain his friendly jovial manner.

I looked at my slightly damp road atlas to see where the best place would be to leave Anthony's company and continue to Dover. It soon became apparent that Swindon was indeed in the south of England, the southwest to be precise, yet my path to Dover was to take me to the southeast.

I followed the best route to Swindon on my map and concluded that we would have to part our ways near Northampton, junction 15A of the M1. Then Anthony could cut across the country to the M40 then onto Swindon. I passed this information to Anthony; with this he pulled up in a nearby service station to look for himself. Anthony agreed, this was the best route for him to take but on looking closer at the road atlas he noticed that there was a truck stop no more than two junctions further from this point. With that he said, that's where he would drop me, as there would be more chance of a lift to Dover from there. I thanked this thoughtful man as we continued on our way.

As we pulled up to the truck stop, after a very enjoyable drive all I could see was rows upon rows of wagons parked up. I wouldn't find it too difficult to get a lift to Dover from here.

I thanked Anthony for all he had done and went to grab my backpack from the back seat.

At that point Anthony said he would approach some wagon drivers for me, to give me the best chance of a lift. So off he went to ask some nearby wagon drivers if they could possibly help me get a lift to Dover.

As I watched this little red-faced man approaching one wagon after another, getting redder and redder with each wagon he approached, he eventually returned to his car looking quite bemused and defeated.

I lifted my backpack and thanked him for trying to talk to the truck drivers while I stepped back from his car.

To my surprise he replied in a loud yet aggressive manner. "Where do you think you're going? You haven't got a chance in hell of getting a lift here there all self-centred egotistical pratts. One of them told me he was going to Dover, but he still wouldn't give you a lift.

" With this he grabbed my backpack, threw it in the back of his car and told me to get in. So, feeling like a naughty school child I sat back in the car.

Whilst we sat in the car, he told me that not one of them drivers had an ounce of common decency and to my surprise he went on to tell me that he would take me to Dover himself! Without a moment to argue he pulled the car away.

This complete stranger was about to drive over two hundred miles out of his way, I told him not to bother, and that I would be sure to get a lift. He didn't stop until we got to Dover ferry port. I asked him for an address so I could send him something for his troubles on my return. With that he handed me a fifty pence peace and said, "promise me one thing, phone your mum and dad to tell them you got to Dover ok". (This man had put my faith back into humanity.)

With that I said thankyou and goodbye, then stood back from the roadside to see (my) little red-faced clown disappear into the distance.

Chapter 3

The Italian Called Walter

When I got over what a complete and utter stranger had just done for me, I approached the ferry port my stomach churned with excitement, knowing I would be on that ferry at long last. I still had enough money for the crossing, but I decided to wait until the following morning, for that was when my last wage was going into the bank and as I was still in England I guess a English cash point would be easier to us than a French one. It was 21:00hours and I was exhausted from the journey, so I made my way to the centre of Dover to try and find a youth hostel or Y.M.C.A. After walking round Dover for a good hour, I found three youth hostels and two Y.M.C.A.s all of which were shut but I wasn't disheartened. I thought to myself, 'I might as well sleep on the promenade seeing as it was only for one night.

I eventually got to the promenade at about 22:30hours. At the same time, I sat down in a promenade shelter a ship's siren wailed across the harbour it scared me out of my skin then it was back to just the gentle lapping of the waves. As I settled in my sleeping bag, I heard footsteps coming from behind the promenade shelter, suddenly a policeman appeared from around the corner, I muttered, "Hello what's wrong officer?"

"Nothing" he replied, "but where is your passport?", so I begrudgingly unwrapped myself from my warm Sleeping bag to face the cold sea breeze and of course to answer the officer's questions. The officer radioed my details through to the station.

At that moment I saw a ferry was docking it seemed to be hovering in the mist with an angelic glow from the deck lights, illuminated it in all its glory.

The policeman brought me out of my dream like state, "Hello" he said, "That's all, but you can only stay here one night is that clear?" I replied, "Yes no problem, I don't want to make a habit of it officer". With that he left and continued his beat.

I must have been asleep no longer than half an hour when I got awoken by a strange squeaking noise which was coming from the distance but coming closer and getting louder. I had become nice and warm in my sleeping bag despite the cold night breeze coming in from the channel, I was not prepared to investigate this strange sound. So, I turned my head to one side and waited for the perpetrator of this nuisance noise to come into view. After five minutes I saw what had been disturbing me.

It was an unexpected sight which walked into view, there before me was a smartly dressed, dark skinned man, not much older than myself.

The man seemed to be struggling with a small, overloaded two wheeled luggage trolley, which he was dragging behind him. With every step he took was then followed by a squeak! The main problem for this unfortunate traveller was, with every three steps he took the little trolley would shake, then fall and topple into a heap beside him. The weary traveller gathered up his things and continued the next three steps.

As the dark-skinned man passed in front of me, I said in a loud, but friendly voice "evening how are you?" Expecting a reply but he never replied.

Now there is several things which upsets me, from people spitting in the street to others dropping their litter. Yet somewhere in the middle is common decency, manners and such like. If someone doth's their cap it is courteous to do so in return.

As this man went on his weary way, I said in a loud, and not too friendly manner "don't speak then you are a fucking Pratt!"

With this the man then turned his head towards me, he looked at my backpack, then turned and started to approach the shelter." Sorry", he said. "I thought you were homeless man, I didn't see your backpack", "where are you going"? he asked in broken English. "Everywhere and nowhere", I replied. I sat up to talk to this foreign man whilst he sat himself down at the opposite end of the shelters bench, on which I was sat, he introduced himself as Walter.

Walter had just landed in the U.K, he had been working on a cruise ship. He said that he'd had enough of the poor wages and long hours so he jumped ship in France, then he came over to Dover on the ferry. Walter was from Italy he showed me his passport, (it was as if he had to prove it to me or something). Whilst we were sat there talking, I got my little block burning camping stove out and began to boil some water. It was to welcome him to England with a nice cup of tea. We started to try to talk to one another, which was a hard enough task as it was.

I spoke English and a little German, he spoke Italian and a little English. I managed to find out he had no money and no cooker, but he did have food. I had money and a cooker but no food. So, we pooled our resources and shared what we had.

Shortly after we had finished our refreshments the policeman returned. Walter had a worried expression on his face, he must have thought the police would send him back to Italy because he had no work permit. After quickly reassuring Walter that he didn't need a work permit to be in England. The policeman checked Walters credentials; it all came back clear. At least I could sleep with a clear conscience, knowing he wasn't a wanted criminal.

after I put my cups away I settled in my sleeping bag once more, as Walter settled at the opposite end of the shelter bench in some blankets he pulled out of one of his bags.

The following morning, I was rudely awoken by the sound of screeching sea gulls gliding around the promenade shelter. I was looking forward to getting to France, but first the bank for my last week's wage, which consisted of 120 British pounds. Walters's bags were still at the end of the bench, but I couldn't see him anywhere. I dragged myself to my feet and sure enough there he was, at the other side of the shelter, he was messing around with a piece of string.

I couldn't make out what he was trying to do with this piece of string, so not wanting to break his concentration I watched to see his plan unfold. He made a loop at both ends of the string, placed his finger through one loop and placed a piece of chewing gum on the other, with this done he stood up and made his way to a nearby sea mine.

This sea mine was an old-world war II mine which had been hollowed out so passersby could put coins in it, for some charity. I watched on in sheer disbelief as Walter lowered the chewing gum into the sea mine and waited.

Eventually the gum stuck to something, as Walter pulled it up, his eyes were shining at the thought of having money, he was like a child with his hand in a candy jar.

Eventually, he pulled a coin out then brought it to me with his fist clenched round whatever he had. He opened his hand and there sat in the centre of his sweaty, shaking hand was a very shiny two pence piece. I told him what he could buy, or more to the point what he couldn't buy with two pence and within a moment his face dropped. I had never seen somebody that sad in my life. Anyway, I was hungry, so I packed my things away, and I headed for a café I had seen when I was looking for the youth hostel, I knew they must do full English breakfasts.

So, there I was walking towards the café with the Italian called Walter grinning like a Cheshire cat next to me, breakfast was on me.

We walked in and I ordered two Full English breakfasts with all the trimmings. Walter and myself sat with our plates piled high, not a word was spoken. But over the pot of tea afterwards, the interrogation began, it felt like I was wearing a sign saying, 'information centre'. I knew Walter wasn't in a good situation when I saw him take the shiny two pence piece out of the sea mine. Yet it felt good to help him.

It was like I was in some way repaying some of the kindness the clown had shown me. There were many questions; the main one which stuck in my mind was when he asked, 'where he could get a job'. I tried to explain about the jobcentre and the Department of social security better known as the DSS, (but this proved to be just too hard), so this gave me half a day to show him what the jobcentre and DSS was all about.

With a slightly more enlightened Walter and a full belly, we made our way through the town to find the jobcentre.

We arrived at the jobcentre just as it was opening so I wasted no time in explaining to this advisor of Walters's unfortunate predicament and his ambition of working in England. We waited in eagerly anticipated for a reply, some answers, some help or anything. This mild-mannered advisor asked just one question, "has Walter got a national insurance number"? This is a number all U.K residents get when they turn sixteen, so a small amount of what you earn can be paid to the government and with this number came your work identity, without this number Walter had no identity or right to work in the eyes of the government".

I asked, "how does he get a national insurance number when he's from Italy"?

The advisor replied, "quite easily all he needs to do is go to the Department of Social Security offices (better known as the DSS) across town and they will issue a temporary number then if you come back here, we will be able to help you more".

I was quite relived for Walter. There seemed to be help for him just around the corner. So, with a map of the town in our hands showing were the DSS was located we made our way to the far side of town, bearing in mind Walter still had his little squeaky trolley with him this made the two-mile walk feel like a hike up a mountain on roller-skates.

As we arrived exhausted to be faced with 'the ticket machine', for those of you who have never had the miss fortune of the ticket machine let me explain, you would have come across supermarket deli's which have a number system were you take a number from the 'ticket machine' and when your number gets called you get faced with a nice, polite shop assistant who wants to serve you and make your experience a happy and enjoyable one.

Well, the DSS ticket machine is very similar to a point. That point being, when your number is called, you don't get that nice friendly face and service, you are faced with a quite subdued person sat behind a bullet proof glass screen.

From this point on it seems that you were a second-class citizen. After sitting there for quite some time on the bolted down moulded plastic seats, Walter's number was called. It took no longer than fifteen minutes to fill out some forms and obtain the all-important national insurance number. We then returned to the jobcentre to find it was closed for lunch to reopen at two o'clock, at that point it was clear to me, I was not going to get my ferry that day.

Once the jobcentre re-opened it didn't take that long for Walter to be processed into the system. They gave him £20.00 and told him to return the next day to obtain details of accommodation which they would pay for. Only for three months and if by the end of that time if he still had no work, he would have to leave the U.K.

With that good news we returned to the town centre as I wasn't going to get the ferry till the next morning so, I decided to see if we could book into the Y.M.C.A, I had seen the previous night. (And so, we did).

After getting a refreshing shower and a clean set of clothes on, we made our way down to the bar. Walter was determined to buy me a beer with his still untouched twenty-pound note.

After a few beers we made our way back to the bunks to get a good night's sleep.

The following morning, I awoke to the hustle and bustle of backpackers getting ready for their onward journeys. After breakfast I walked with Walter to the jobcentre, it didn't seem to take long at all Walter was given a date he would have accommodation and a health worker to advise him from there on. So, with that, it was time to continue my adventure, it felt that I was releasing a bird back into the wild as I said goodbye and good luck to my Italian friend.

Walter offered me some money for helping him, but I told him "I don't take payment for favours" and with a smile I went on my way to the ferry port. I don't know where Walter is now, but I don't think I will ever forget him. One thing he told me in perfect English was "If you slam a door behind you, it is hard to open it again". I was to learn that this could not be truer.

A friend of mine told me if I could find a truck driver at the port who was willing to take me across then I wouldn't have to pay for the ferry crossing, a free passage sounded good to me.

While I was walking around the ferry terminal trying to find the truck driver's lounge a female customs officer approached me and said "Mr Winter!" I don't know how she knew my name to this day, but she explained to me that I shouldn't have been in that area, then she kindly pointed me to the foot passenger entrance. I asked her how much the ticket would be, and she told me it was twenty pounds single to Calais. So, I was forced to buy a ticket to France.

While I was in the departure lounge, I met several other travellers all of whom were staying in France. They all had return tickets for some reason and when I asked why it all became clear, that a promotional day return was a special ticket for only £1. So, they got to the other side and either threw their return ticket away or more commonly sold it to someone else wishing to get home. As you might expect, finding this out upset me, not that they were ripping off the ferry company, just that nobody told me about this deal.

I tried not to dwell on paying much more than anyone else and made my way to the top deck to watch the white cliffs of Dover disappear off the horizon, there was a group of five backpacker's also up there for much the same reason to say farewell to good old blighty and hello to Europe.

Chapter 4
Paris France

After a gentle crossing, I arrived in Calas about midday. After disembarking I was faced by a large expanse of flat land, not one hill in sight, the land was packed with stacks of shipping containers waiting to be loaded for their ongoing voyages.

From here on I would be able to use the European rail ticket and my new destination would be a little town called Menden near Dortmund Germany. There were several reasons for this, I was based in Menden whilst I was in the army so, I knew the area quite well. But the main reason had to be, I was running low on funds after helping Walter, so I needed to find work as soon as possible.

I Had some friends who used to live in Menden, and I was hoping they would still be there, some 2 ½ years after I had left the forces. I was sure that they could help me find work, if I could find them. Once out of the port I stopped a small chubby balding man for directions to the train station, I've always tried to speak other languages when I'm a guest in other people's countries, just out of courtesy but my French was well, very limited.

I knew how to say "yes, no and have you any work" in French, but my German was better. So, I tried to communicate in German with this man, this man's facial expiration changed, he must have been German I thought to myself.

He looked me up and down then took a deep breath and said in a clear London accent "that's all I fucking need, a fucking BOX HEAD" then he pushed me aside and carried on his way muttering under his breath.

Out of all the people I could have stopped, I had to stop the stereo typical booze cruse larger lout as far as exports go this type of export we could do without.

I eventually found the train station without any more interactions with anybody.

I found myself stood in front of the flickering train timetable boards, which might as well have been in Latin for all the good it did .90% of the destinations seemed to be going to Paris.

As I looked around I noticed everyone around me was also looking at the flickering boards with the same blank expression on their faces, so I was not alone.

At that moment a young man approached me, he said very slowly "do, you, speak, English,".
He was another lost English man, with that I replied, "I speak English quite well". At this news he seemed quite relieved and went onto explain that he was just as lost as I was. so, with that we made our way to the information desk.

It turned out that I would have to go to Paris first then onto Düsseldorf and finally it would be an overnight wait on the station platform for yet another train to Menden.

The young lost English man was a lot happier knowing where he was going.

He was also going to Germany a place called *Osnabruck* further south than where I was going, but he would also need to go via Paris and Düsseldorf and then a quick change to *Osnabruck his destination.*

So, it seemed I had a temporary travelling companion and we had one hour to kill until the train to Paris was to depart.

There was a nearby bar, we could hear music, so we stepped through the door to soak up the atmosphere and taste some local refreshments. After talking for a while, it became apparent that this young man was a solider called Simon from Newcastle. He was on his way back to his Army camp in *Osnabruck* and then he was to start a 6-month tour of duty in Northern Ireland. When I first asked him where he was going, he told me he was visiting friends, because all soldiers are told to be warier when travelling back to their Army camps as the risk of a terrorist attack was very real.

Now there are several things that make soldiers stand out from the crowd like a sore thumb especially to an ex- soldier like me, from there regimental hair cut to the way they walked. After telling Simon more about myself and where I was based for three years he seemed to open-up and relax a lot more, he was quite concerned about going to Northern Ireland, I tried to reassure him as my brother had been there two years previously when the violence was considerably worse (and you are only here the bad stories on TV, don't you).

I was sure Simon would be fine and there was no point in worrying about things which were out of his control. Anyway, he was still on Holiday, so I changed the subject and invented a game to pass the time called "Spot the good-looking French girl" to take his mind off his job for a while.

It seemed that the time passed in a blink of an eye, when we made our way to the platform to board our train and what a train it was.

To our surprise there in front of us was the one and only bullet high speed train, shimmering in white with its space age aerodynamic pointed nose, the first time seeing this train was breath taking, like giggling schoolboys we boarded our space age train.

After we stored are luggage in the overhead compartments and sat back in our plush leather reclining seats, the first thing we both noticed wasn't the lack of noise coming from the supercharged engines, what we did noticed was the underside of the polished glass luggage shelves running down the full length of the carriage above our heads, the reason for this was clear, you could say as clear as a mirror.

As we tilted our Seats back, we could see the reflection of everyone sat in front of us, that included all the beautiful women that France had to offer. As it was November and the trains heating was on, one by one the ladies unbuckled and stowed there thick winter coats to revel little miniskirts and low-cut tops and we had a bird's eye view. So, we sat there in our self-made heaven for a full hour and a half, until too our dismay, we pulled into central Paris train station where we were to change trains to Düsseldorf.

As we had quite a while to wait for our ongoing train, we decided to have a quick look at Paris outside the station. To our astonishment all we could see was yet more beautiful French girls, so with that we had to change are challenge from find the beautiful French girl to find the ugly French girl. After spending all of our spare time looking for this rare illusive unfindable creature, we had to make our way back to the train station content that there was no such thing as an Ugly French girl in Paris.

In no time we were on our way to Düsseldorf, on a less impressive train as before but the evening was closing in with the realisation that we would be going are separate ways soon. Many paths might cross but very few continue to the same destination.

As we pulled into Dusseldorf, I knew I had a long night ahead of me, so I said goodbye to Simon the soldier and made my way to the information desk to find out which platform I needed for the following morning.

I decided I would wait at the platform all night so not to miss the connecting train. When I got to my platform, I found that Simon was waiting there, unfortunately his train had been delayed so we kept each other company. Simon asked if I wanted to spend the night at his barracks in Osnabruck instead of having to wait on a cold platform all night. It made more sense to take Simon up on his generous offer, than huddling in the cold air all night, so I graciously accepted Simon's kind offer.

I would have to be up early the next morning because Simon was needing to be on parade to commence his tour of duty by 07:00hrs. This journey wasn't as entertaining as the first, but we were too tired to notice.

We arrived in Osnabruck some hours later. We grabbed our things and made our way to the stairway off the platform. As we approached the bottom of the stairway, I glanced up to see a large dark-skinned man standing at the top of the stairs, then without warning this man pulled a pistol out from under his jacket and pointed the barrel towards us.

Within a split second our instinct and military training kicked in, are movements were synchronized. Simon and I dropped to the floor and rolled in opposite directions my heart was racing like a trapped mouse waiting for the darkness to fall. Then in a fraction of a second my life really did flash before my eyes from my first action man toy age 4 to the situation I found myself in.

In army basic training everyone is told," if you come under fire to drop, roll, take cover, and then return fire", in a battlefield situation this is fine. But it was chillingly apparent that this was no battlefield situation.

As I laid there waiting to hear the shot, a very selfish thought was running through my mind over and over again, all I could think was "shoot him not me" self-preservation is a strange and humbling experience.

All within a second the shot was fired, with a pop, and a realisation that I was not hit. I glanced over to Simon who lay there quite still he turned and looked at me, then we both looked up the stairway towards the gun man who was on the floor at the top of the stairs holding his stomach , not in pain, but in fits of laughter this man was no more than a practical joker with a replica pistol just trying to scare the young soldiers who were coming back to their Army camp.

With that we both got to our feet and for some reason which baffles me to this day, we didn't kick the living shit out of this man. We just stood up, grabbed our bags, and continued our way up the stairway an out of the station, not a word spoken. This trance like state lasted until we were safely stood in the fresh cold air on the pavement outside the train station. Then realisation and acknowledgement of what had just happened came over us.

All we could do was laugh. After talking about what was going through our minds at the time it became apparent that Simon was thinking and hoping the same as me, "shoot him not me". Self-preservation is truly a funny thing!

Once we had composed ourselves. We found a phone box and Simon phoned his camp and had us picked up by the duty driver who dropped us off at Simons barrack block for a well-deserved rest. As soon as we got to the accommodation block, I found a piece of floor in the corridor and rolled out my sleeping bag to settle down for the night.

I was woken by the soundtrack from the film 'good morning, Vietnam!' playing at full volume. From a room to the left of the corridor all I heard was "IT'S 'O' SIX HUNDRED HOURS WHAT DOES THE 'O' STAND FOR... 'O' MY GOD IT'S EARLY.

Suddenly all hell broke loose, all the room doors opened at the same time, and it was panic stations.

One person was shouting, "where's my boot?" Another person couldn't find his webbing. There were about thirty soldiers waiting for the toilets at once, and where was I? That's right, lying right in the doorway to the washroom and toilets. So, they moved me to one side and all I heard was "Who the hell's in the sleeping bag ?".

I replied, "Ask the soldier in that room, he's called Simon from Newcastle". It turned out all of them were from Newcastle. I got out of my sleeping bag to explain myself.

I was relieved to find they took my presence light heartedly and when they had no more questions, they recommenced pushing their way to the toilets. Soon after this I gathered my things together, thanked Simon for his hospitality and wished all the lads the very best of luck for their tour of duty, I made my way to the main gate and then onto the train station, to start my last leg to Menden to hopefully find some help from my old friends.

Chapter 5
Friends from times gone by

The journey to Menden took me via Dortmund, this was only a quick change of trains as the morning rush hour had commenced. I was eager to see if anyone there could help me find work. I pulled into Menden train station; my first point of call would be the Army camp of 50 missile regiment Royal Artillery.

After a brisk mile and a half walk in the bitter freezing morning air, I turned the last corner to see my camp gates in front of me. To my surprise there were no guards, there was no regimental signs, all there seemed to be, was an eerie silence, as the last of the autumn leaves gathered at the entrance. It became apparent that this camp had become a casualty of military cutbacks, deserted and for sale.

After resting a while at the gates of the camp where I once stood on guard, I had a handful of places I could try in the local area were if luck was on my side, I might find some old friends who could point me in the right direction for work.

I had an English friend called Charlie who lived here with his wife and a German friend called Ingo who last time I saw him, was at college and lived with his parents. But we all had one place in common, and that place was 'mama and papas' this was a bar I used to frequently visit, a short walk from the camp.

The real name of the bar translated into ' The Long Bar ' Zu langer Teka. We all called it "mama and papa's" because of the friendly landlord and landlady, they came not from Germany but from Romania sometime in the 1940's, but they had hearts of gold. They were in their late 80's well over retirement age last time I saw them.

So, I put my backpack on and made my way to mama and papa's hoping for a change in fortune. I didn't expect anyone to recognise me, but I couldn't have been more wrong. I ducked my head as I walked through the small wooden door of the bar, I notice everything had changed from the colour of the walls, to where the fruit machine was placed. My heart dropped through the floor just as the army camp had changed so had my beloved bar.

I raised my head and glanced to where once papa had sat with his receding hair line and cheerful toothless smile, while chewing on hot chillies and playing a German dice game called shock speal. He never played for money only for drinks. To my delight I was faced with yes, the same cheerful red-faced toothless smile I had grown to love once more.

A glow came over his face as he nearly choked on a small chilli pepper when he saw me stood weighted down with my rucksack in his doorway. At that moment he stood up and shouted in a warm and friendly voice "Bernie". This was a nick name he had given me, because my last name is Winter and the only winter he knew of, was 'Bernie Winters and snorbitz' an old comedy act from England. My spirits rose as I knew I was among friends once more. It felt more like a 20-year reunion than a 2-year reunion, but what a reunion it was.

I ordered a beer, but papa refused to take my money and every time I got to the bottom of my glass, he would re-fill it I told him to take some payment, but all he said, "In very broken English" was, "you are my guest". With that mama appeared from the kitchen, carrying a platter of hot dogs and burger for all to sample. Now papa could speak only a small amount of English, yet he could understand a lot and I could only speak a small amount of German, but also, I could understand a lot.

As for mama she was never interested in speaking or learning English, why should she after all, I wasn't in England, and neither was she. But when mama wanted to be understood she was. She may have looked like a little frail old woman but there was no mistaking she was the boss of that Bar.

After speaking with mama and papa about my friends Charlie and Ingo, they could tell me very little. They had seen Charlie about a month ago and Ingo popped in now and again. I remembered were Charlie and his wife lived so I left my bag behind the bar with mama and made my way to their flat a short distance from the bar. Walking without my bag made me feel lighter than air itself. As my funds were getting low, I needed some work, so I couldn't wait to see Charlie once more. I got to the flat, rang the bell and between me ringing the bell and someone answering I was trying to think what to say.

When the door opened, I was speechless, there in front of me stood a stranger. I thought to myself, who the hell's he?
Then I heard a voice from the past, it was Charlie's wife.

She came to the door with a shocked expression on her face. I said, "Is Charlie here?"

"No" she replied. It turned out that they had separated a year after I left the Army and the man who answered the door was her new boyfriend. It seemed that I was in the bad books for merely mentioning Charlie's name.

Not wanting to upset or intrude I decided to go back to mama's and papas with my options steadily dwindling.

When I returned to the bar papa had just appeared at the bottom of the stairs from there private accommodation above the bar looking redder than usual and quite out of breath. I asked what was wrong and he replied," nothing just your bag is very heavy". Then he went on to explain that mama insisted that he was to take my bag to the spare room at the very top of the building up three very narrow stairways, as I was to stay there that night. I thanked him and mama as he poured me yet another beer and then got out the dice and cups to play a few rounds of shock speal.

After a few more beers and a few more games I made my way to my room to rest my head.

I awoke the next morning and as I opened my eyes, it let in a stream of light, which came through the small frost covered south facing bedroom window, at the foot of my bed. Due to the glistening winter frost clinging to the windowpane despite its size, it had still managed to distribute the light evenly around the small attic room like a prism. As the light hit my awakening eye's, it seemed to bore deep into my brain with a sudden and siring pain. It seemed after 22 and a bit years alive I was experiencing my first and not to be my last hangover.

As I took my first deep breath of the cold morning air, I could feel the air particles hitting my tongue and the back of my throat, with my exhale a flow of my breath became visible in a cloud of crystallised vapor, as the little moister I had in my mouth was dissipated into the room.

After several minutes lying there feeling the gradual warmth of the sun fighting its way into the room, I made my way to my feet to see what the day had in store for me. Mama and papa were already up and about, doing there morning chores, as I walked into the bar area slightly worse for wear. Mama sat me down with papa and brought out some bacon rolls and coffee then I went onto explain what my plans were today.

The plan was to try and find Ingo, as I knew his English was extremely good and he could explain to me how the job market worked in Germany as I explained to Walter in the UK how our system worked. After thanking my attentive, generous hosts, I gathered my things and grabbed my Rucksack and with a hug and a handshake I was on my way refreshed and ready for the day. I started my search at Ingo's parents' house this seemed to be the best place to start looking. To my surprise my memory didn't fail me and I found their house quite easily.

There seemed to be no change here, the same front gate, the same gnomes and wishing well in the garden. As I rang the bell I saw Ingo's farther coming to the door, now Ingo's sister can speak English and his Mother, but his Farther, well no matter how much I tried I could not understand him, he spoke very fast with a slightly different dialect .All I could do was apologise for my lack of understanding and ask if Ingo or Ingo's sister was there, with that the answer was "no", I asked when would they be back and he replied " komm morgen fruh wieder " come back in the morning. I thanked him and made my way to the centre of town.

Paul, my friend back in Yorkshire, wasn't due to be in Germany for at least two more weeks I was down to my last 50 Deutsche Mark, but I still had my rail ticket. As I got to the centre of Menden to my joy and dismay came the snow, this was not the English snow I was used to.

It was the snow you see on TV, proper snowflakes were dancing before me, no less than an inch across with their pure white arms spread out swirling and floating on the breeze like a ballet being performed in shear silent's, just for me. It took no more than a minute for the first flakes of snow to carpet the ground and roof tops around me, this is what Christmas should look like.

As I walked aimlessly through the centre of town, pondering over the idea of returning to England I gathered my thoughts and I made my way to the marketplace, I found myself sat on my rucksack on the church steps overlooking the Christmas market. All the market stalls were covered in the white virgin snow and illuminated by multi coloured fairy lights.

The sound of carols echoing from one of the stalls in the distance, the smell of Christmas spices wafted past me on the breeze coming from a nearby stall, which was selling glühwein, a typical German Christmas drink made from wine and spices, similar to mulled wine but with a unique taste of its own.

After paying 3DM for a mug of glühwein, I sat myself down once more on the church steps to sip my warming wine and soaked in this amazing atmosphere as dusk started to fall. If I could have frozen that moment in time I would have done, for at that moment, not one negative thought entered my mind, I was indeed living in the moment!

I finished my drink an as I felt the warmth disappearing from the mug I had been clenching, I had little time to decide where to go from here. Even though mama and papa would have probably welcomed me in for another night I didn't wish to overstay my welcome.

I had the equipment with me to survive a bit of snow, so I made my way out of town to find a suitable place to set up camp. After walking a few miles, I came across some open land in a secluded area, after clearing some snow with the side of my boots I pitched my tent. The snow had stopped, and the sky was clear as I climbed into my tent and kicked off my boots. I knew the temperature would drop during the night, so I changed my socks and put on another layer of clothes, then dragged myself into my sleeping bag and tied the hood around my head so not even my nose was open to the cold. My sleeping bag was tested to -20 so I thought I would be ok!

After tossing and turning for a good few hour, I came to the conclusion that the temperature must have dropped to less than
-20 as I was feeling the cold despite the layers of clothing. My teeth were uncontrollably chattering, I was aware that this was a way the body warned people that hypothermia was just around the corner.

With that I started to strip, yes that's right in the tent I took off all my clothes down to my boxershorts, this act alone heated my body as the movement within the tent generated heat, then as I put one layer of clothes on after the other, trapping warm air next to my skin I knew this would only help for a short period of time so I quickly packed my things away and made my way back into the town centre, to look for a more suitable shelter. With my fingertips hurting from the cold, as I approached the town centre once more.

I saw a sign for some public toilets on the side of a small stone building. I made my way up some narrow stairs then as I walked in the doorway of these toilets the lights automatically came on, there in front of me was a hand washer and drying unit all in chrome with that I threw my bag to the floor and place my cold hands into the unit to feel warm water being dispensed onto my cold hands.

With first a shock from the water and then a soothing sensation from the hot air blowing over my wet hands I gradually regained full feeling back to my fingers.

This was a very clean public toilet not like any you would find in the UK, once I got my camping stove out it was quite warm, so I decided not to brave the cold once more but to stay where I was and wrap myself back in my sleeping bag.

Before I knew it the morning was upon me, I was glad to feel and see the sun's rays coming through the frosted glass windows of the toilet block. Once packed It didn't take long for the hustle and bustle of town life to start soon after the sunrise. At that moment I headed back to Ingo's parents' house to hopefully meet up with him once more. After a cold morning stroll uphill, I rang the bell and waited in anticipation.

Ingo's mother answered the door, she was the first person not to recognise me. I asked if Ingo was there, she told me that he didn't live there anymore he had left home. She gave me a piece of paper with his new address and telephone number on it. I didn't know what to expect it to say, knowing my luck probably Stuttgart or Berlin, which are both at least two hundred miles away. But I was lucky, it said Unna which was a neighbouring town. Five minutes by bus and thirty minutes by foot in good weather. So, I did it on foot. For a good reason, a very good reason, I only had limited funds I was down to my last 40 deutsche mark (approximately £15)!

The walk was a long cold slog, uphill for most of the journey, I asked directions along the way to ensure I didn't get lost this time. To my delight and relief, I found the address I was given in good time. It was quite a formidable building; it was a dark grey stone building with a wide grand curved stone stairway leading to a small porch at the centre of this three-story square block of flats.

As I stood Infront of the named plates and buzzers, in the porch, the door to the building was a-jar and I could hear voices coming from the hallway. I knocked and pushed the door open and there before me was a skinhead. If I didn't know better, he could have been a member of the Hitler youth. He had bright blue eyes very short cut blonde hair, wearing German army para boots and urban camouflaged combat trousers. He could have looked intimidating but for one thing, he was about 5ft.5 inch tall. This man was talking to another person at the first flat. To my surprise the other person was Ingo.

I didn't notice it was him at first, the last time I saw Ingo he wasn't as tall as me or as broad. As soon as he saw me at his doorway, he looked at me in sheer disbelief while saying "Bernie is that you"? I must have looked like a sight for saw eyes, as I was unshaven cold, wet and possibly just a bit smelly. To my astonishment Ingo had turned into a six-foot seven monster.

He dreamt of being a world class goalkeeper and he was in a local team last time I had seen him it turned out this had not changed he was still striving to be that goalkeeper. I suppose his size would be an advantage.

Ingo invited me in, and I told him my predicament, he said I could stay for as long as I wanted, I was reluctant to take his help as I did feel a bit embarrassed at needing help so soon on my travels, but I had no choice.

Once I had jumped into the shower had a shave and grabbed something clean and dry clothes from my backpack, I looked more like my old self. Ingo and I talked till the early hours, so we were both up to date regarding our lives what had changed and remained the same. He was another German who liked to celebrate. The next night I met all his new friends and I managed to forget all my problems for that one night.

I stayed at his flat for two weeks as the holiday season had just started, everyone was off work and in the party mood which made finding work near impossible and saving any of my money defiantly impossible. It would have been rude not to join in on the celebrations and I was sure I would find some work soon.

I phoned Paul soon after the first week I was at Ingos to find out when he was coming over on holiday to see his mother. When he found out my situation, he said Steve his mum's boyfriend might know of some available work as a labourer, seeing as he was a British bricklayer over there for the high wages offered. We arranged to meet at Paderborn in two days' time. I knew it was a good 50 miles to Paderborn from where I was, so I gave myself two days to get there.

I intended to save as much funds as possible so it would have to be back to hitchhiking were ever I could until I could use my rail ticket that is.

I packed my things all dry and clean ready for my next challenge. I said goodbye to Ingo and thanked him for kindly lending me 100 deutschmarks to see me through. I had his address and was determined to repay his kindness. But for now, that would have to wait.

Chapter 6
German Xmas the Yorkshire way

To my amazement it didn't even take a day to get to Paderborn, so I decided to break the news of Pauls pending arrival to his mum, who I had never met in my life but had heard a lot about.

I got to the residential caravan site where she was living and there, I saw a woman feeding some ducks on a nearby lake, so I asked if she knew Cathy from Yorkshire, as I've come from Yorkshire. She said, "What a coincidence, I came from Yorkshire too" as she carried on her way, laughing to herself.

After I caught up with her, she introduced herself as Paul's mum, I explained that Paul was coming over she replied in sheer disbelief "I will believe it when I see it". That's when I found out he had never left England before. I walked with her to her caravan, this wasn't any normal caravan it looked like your standard 6 berth caravan with a very large horning attached to it.

Once we got past the zipped doorway of the horning, standard went out the window. First there was a full size wooden front door and once you stepped through, it opened to a stunning wood panelled room with a crackling log burning stove on a stone hearth in the far lefthand corner. It was like stepping into a wilderness cabin a very comfortable cabin, at that.

The caravan to the back of the horning was draped with Trible pattered blankets which only left the doorway to the caravan in view. It was a standard 6 berth which had all the normal amenities, it was all super insulated for the German winters it was a brilliant way to live, the rent was low as was the running costs.

Paul, my childhood friend, had told me about his mums' travels and by the photos and books littering her shelves she was indeed well travelled.

We were settling down with a cup of tea in front of the log burner stove, we chatted for a while and I asked about work and Cath told me her boyfriend (Steve) needed a labourer after the holidays, but Steve was away till the new year. It was the 21st of December, and everybody was in the middle of the Christmas celebrations. As in Germany Christmas starts from the 6th of December so it's a party Month.

Cath grabbed out some spare blankets and pulled out the sofa bed, about 3 feet away from the roaring crackling log burner. Then she said good night and made her way to her bed in the caravan. I had an amazing relaxing night sleep one of the best for a long time.

The next morning, we were both up early I felt recharged and energised, ready for whatever the world could throw at me. Cathy went to feed her ducks and she was still saying she didn't believe her son was coming.

I had been friends with Paul since secondary school he was raised by his grandparents on a small farm in North Yorkshire. He was pulled out of private education and was placed into mainstream school after his parents separated and he became my classmate and a very good friend, if he said he was coming he was coming!

The coach he was coming on was due to arrive around midday, so we made our way to great him off the bus, the torture bus, named after the long and torturous journey it took to get to Paderborn as its route goes from the north of England across to holland through France and a little bit of Belgium before arriving in Germany and onto Paderborn.

I didn't envy my friend on his first trip out of England as he was 6 feet + tall and leg room on the torture bus was an afterthought a very distant afterthought.

As everything in Germany was so punctual, it didn't come as a surprise that the bus turned up, just on time. Then we were faced by the very weary looking travellers stumbled off the bus, one by one, not one smiling face in sight, you could see the life force drained from their souls, it seemed the torture bus had taken more victims.

It was quite easy to identify the Yorkshire man as he was the only one wearing a flat cap and big boots ready for anything or so he thought.

After Paul had rested for a while, the nights celebrations began once more. Paul's mum invited some of the neighbours around which consisted of mostly German friends, they told us about a few German traditions which included of course drinking, eating and surprisingly, hunting pigs in the woods. The germens even had a yearly festival, where they would walk into the woods with only a single, six-foot-long spear and a small knife to do battle against these wild pigs.

This gave me and Paul an idea. Please remember that we had consumed a substantial amount of alcohol, and some decisions should not be made under these conditions, so it wasn't a sound mind what said, "should we go on a pig hunt?" apparently these pigs were in the neighbouring woodland.

It took us seconds to get ourselves together in a frenzy of excitement at getting a pig, we didn't have the intention of killing the little pigs, we intended to maybe keep one as a pet.

So off we went with a few beers in our hands obviously, we armed ourselves with some non-lethal weapons which consisted of a big rubber mallet, and the first thing I grabbed was a big plastic bottle which I filled with water to add some weight to my weapon to hopefully render the little pig unconscious, which seemed like a good idea.

After climbing over some walls, through some brambles we were on the lookout. It was luck more than judgement that it was a full moon, and the visibility was quite good with the iridescent light of moon being sufficient to allow a pig to stand out.

After wondering around for a while first being as quiet as a mouse to try and hear the odd snort from our pet pig, we then changed our tactic and tried calling them but after a while "here piggy here piggy" just didn't work either.

Then in the distance we saw what can only be described as the beast from hell it was like a pig but covered in dark black hair, it stood three times higher than a normal farmyard pig and above all it was armed, with big sharp tusks and teeth not what we expected.

Now in hindsight it would have been a good idea to slowly move away unnoticed, but hindsight is a wonderful thing and the human instinct to survive kicked in, within a split second we both ran, not noticing how much noise we were making, at this time the hunter became the hunted. We could hear a stampeding hog with its tusks ripping through the undergrowth behind us.

The only sound which drowned out the pursuing beast was the sound of my heart beating out of my chest as it became apparent that I was running out of energy and speed, so I aimed for the nearest tree and I climbed, I climbed like a monkey I only stopped once I was a good 20 ft up in the branches of a quite spectacular oak tree.

I looked down and saw the hog from hell very upset snorting at the base of the tree, a noise in the undergrowth distracted it and it seemed to move on to investigate. I noticed Paul hanging out of a tree about 30 meters away at the opposite side of the track in the direction that the hog had headed but we were both safe and recovering on our chosen branches. Like proper Yorkshire men we both had a bear safely stowed away in our pockets so once we were refreshed and confident our little piggy had moved way, we admitted defeat and made our way back to the caravan.

Cathy was excited as Steve, her partner, was returning the following day, they had explained a little about what Steve was like. But after meeting him, I would describe him as the gentle giant, his hand could close around an apple the same as most people can do with an acorn. He must have been not far off seven foot tall with a slight hippy look to him he liked a drink and the odd smoke.

I worked for Steve for a few weeks as a labourer, my main job was to keep Steve and his friend stocked up with bricks and cement so they could get much more done in a day and earn more money. I was paid a gratuity by each bricklayer I supplied the bricks to so the harder I worked the more I carried the more I could earn, but this work did take a toll on my health I must have pulled muscles I didn't even know I had.

But on a positive note, I was more physically fit as I ever had been. But it was only temporary work. I managed to save a small amount of money to travel with. So, with work slowing down it was time to move on. I decided to return to Ingo's to repay him the money he had lent me and post some money through mama's and papa's door to cover just a bit of the beer I had drunk there. I said goodbye to Steve and Cath, and I was on my way back to Unna then Menden once again this time with a smile on my face and money in my pocket.

From here on I was traveling by my thumb as the rail ticket had expired.

Ingo offered to let me stay over the weekend, which gave me the opportunity to plan my route and where I was to go from there. That night I went drinking for the last time with Ingo and his skinhead friend.

Chapter 7
A Close Call

Monday morning came quicker than I would have liked, my plan was to continue looking for work on my way back towards England as all my contacts and options in Germany had dried up. I was hoping I would find work on the way to lengthen my stay in Europe. I had two pounds of luncheon meat and a lump of cheese in my backpack, which I expected to last one or two days and to save the little money I had left I was back to hitchhiking. It was a frosty January morning but once I hit the road, I warmed up quickly it wasn't long before I got my first lift, it seemed luck was on my side.   I got picked up by a large bald man who was driving an old grey Citroen with a red and white Belgian registration plate.

 I placed my rucksack behind the front passenger seat and jumped in next to the lone driver, I thanked him for stopping and explained that I was wanting to make my way back towards the UK but I was looking for work if he knew any ware.

I was surprised and quite relieved to find that this large balding man spoke English very well he was a very friendly and talkative character, and he was heading back to Belgium which would leave me a lot closer to the UK.

After a short period of time sat with this man certain things started to concern me, he was friendly, very friendly. While he was talking to me, he started touching and rubbing his upper thigh and groin region and seemed to be getting more and more excited at having company in his car. After driving no more than a half an hour with this man it became apparent that he wanted more than just company on this journey, if you know what I mean.

This became more obvious when he turned off the motorway for a break, but he drove straight passed the service station and told me he knew a better place to stop, alarm bells were ringing in my head.

I was still hoping that he was going to pull up at a cheaper wagon stop or something but when he turned off the main road and headed down a dark forest road this was a nightmare coming true.

He pulled up under the trees and started undoing his belt and top button of his trousers. There was no doubt in my mind, of this man's intentions. I had not given this man any reason to believe I was wishing this to happen. Within a spilt second, I gained clarity of what I should do next, with one single motion I reached down to my ankle lifted my jeans and grabbed my survival ankle knife.

As I stated before I was prepared for any eventuality or situation, as I sat back in my seat, I raised my knife and rested it on the drivers lap with the point precariously situated towards his genitals.

In that second there was a calm atmosphere and the excitement the driver had dissipated in an instant.

I told this man to start the car and take me back to the service station if he valued his health, so with his belt still loosened, his top button unfastened and zip down he drove me back to the service station.

Once we arrived I had this sleezy individual hand me the car keys, while I grabbed my things then I threw his keys on the floor outside the car and made my escape.

 I watched from a safe distance, as the driver recovered his keys and sped off into the distance. Out of any situation I may have found myself in I didn't expect this, me being a man and all, not meaning to sound sexiest or anything I would never encourage a Woman of my age to travel alone because of the inherent risks that may pose.

While I was thanking my lucky stars that I was away from this predator the heavens opened and I found myself in familiar territory lost somewhere in Germany no were near Belgium, but at least I was safe.

After working out where I was, I started heading towards the nearest city called Koln, a nearby sign said Koln was 50km away, so I grabbed my things and hoped I would find better fortune there, my logic was more people more chance of a lift towards the water's edge. The bad weather seemed to be following me and it wasn't long till I decided to set camp for the night and just write off the day and put it down to experience and not a very good experience.

I set off early the following morning, the sun was breaking through the clouds, and I was soon picked up by a lovely German family on their way to visit relatives in a place called Bergisch Gladbach, which happened to be on the far side of Koln. At long last I had a break in my fortune.

The family dropped me off in the middle of the city called Köln, a very beautiful city with a magnificent awe-inspiring medieval cathedral, which casts a dark shadow over the train station in the centre of the city.

After bidding the family farewell I absorbed the sights and smells coming from a street vendors cart, selling German sausages of all types, the tantalizing smell seemed to follow me around the cobbled streets of this mediaeval city.

I gazed across a car park and to my surprise I saw a van with 'Sheffield rent-a-van England' written on the side. A thought of failure came into my mind as if I were to get a lift from here straight back to the UK, I would have failed. But excepting my fait would be the only thing I could do at this point, so I waited by the van as I knew there must be a driver somewhere. While I waited, I looked in my bag to see the last of the luncheon meat lying at the bottom and I hesitated no longer. As I ate it, I imagined it was a juicy German sausage and I could taste all the spices you would expect tricking my mind and my taste buds.

After I had finished the luncheon meat it became apparent, just as it started to rain once more, that there wasn't anybody coming back to the van that night.

Chapter 8
The Hard Work
Starts Here

As the rain turned into a downpour I looked around for some shelter, I saw some circus wagons through the haze of the rain. I thought I could sit out the rain under one of the parked trailers and possibly ask the circus people the best way back to the motorway. As I approached the circus trailers, I noticed a young woman wearing a hooded overcoat stood next to the wagons. I asked, "Do you speak English" then I said "Do you speak German" I thought it would be obvious that she would speak German seeing as I was, after all in Germany.

To my amazement she didn't speak either then suddenly, this strange woman started dragging me towards the biggest caravan situated in the middle of the circus ground. She knocked on the door of this very bright large luxurious caravan, with that the door swung open.

There in front of me was a big German man with blonde hair and a rounded red chubby face, he must have stood six foot six at least and he had hands the size of shovels a true tower of a man.

It became apparent that this was the boss, and even he couldn't speak English. With what little German I knew I asked, "Where is the motorway?". Then to my surprise he asked me if I would like some work and if I had a driving license.

I told him I had a license and that I would like some work in my best broken German. Well, I was cold, wet and I had run out of food, so this opportunity was literally too good to pass up.

The boss then pointed to a small old fashioned gypsy style caravan with wooden wheels and wooden steps leading to a door at the rear he said "sleep there" in German so things were looking up I had a bed for the night at least.

I opened the door and was faced with an old man on bended knees loading up an old wood burning stove. He turned towards me and smiled with a weathered face and the few teeth he had left in his mouth. This man looked like he had been through a lot in his life, he pointed at the top bunk of a bunk bed which was bolted to the wall of the caravan. So that's where I placed my bag before I huddled in front of the log burner to dry off my soaking wet clothes.

The old man only spoke polish and no matter how many times I told him I didn't understand he just kept on talking. So, I sat there for a good few hours just nodding my head when I thought it was appropriate. Eventually I called it a night and got myself comfortable for an unexpected peaceful night's sleep with the mutterings of the old polish man disappearing as I drifted off into my dream world.

The morning came seemingly quicker than usual. I got dressed and opened the door to be blinded by the morning sun. When my eyes became accustomed to the light, I saw rows and rows of wagons in front of me all of which had 'Circus Barelli' painted across them in big blue, yellow and red letters.

That's when it struck me, I had never seen a real circus before, or if I had I was too young to remember. My mind was brought back into the circus wagon by the whistle of an old tin kettle boiling on the top of the wood burning stove, as the old polish man was making coffee.

We had a coffee and a crusty roll then the polish man put on his thread worn tweed jacket which had been drying over the back of a rickety old chair and beckoned me to follow him to see what the boss had in mind for me.

We headed to the centre of the circus ground where the boss's caravan was located and we were not alone, there must have been about 15 to 20 people gathered in a few groups near the caravan. They were all talking their own languages some were smartly dressed, and others would look more at home in a cardboard box under a bridge. There in front of me was the full spectrum of the circus community from the valuable artists to the lowest of low, I would find myself being in the latter group.

As soon as the bosses caravan door opened everyone fell silent to listen to whatever he had to say. Now the Boss only spoke German, so anyone who could understand German needed to explain to the others what jobs were to be allocated starting with the artists and then working down in order of value or seniority. As soon as a group was given a task, they left the area to commence whatever tasks they were given or to discuss the tasks in whatever language they spoke, it seemed quite an organised and effective operation.

I was still stood with the old polish man who had joined a larger group of younger polish men. None of which had a smile on their face. While the jobs were allocated to the other groups, there was circus performers, animal trainers, and a large group of Germans wearing work boots and warm jackets. Later I found these people to be relatives of the boss and fundamental to the circus.

Eventually we were the only group left and the boss started speaking. I could understand a little, but he spoke so fast and seemed to expect us to understand first time, as the new boy I kept my head down and waited until the polish men went to move off to their allocated workplaces and so I followed closely. I had only taken two steps and then I heard the Boss shout English man, with that I stopped in my tracks. He went on to ask me for my driving license, so I fumbled around in my pockets and pulled out my passport and driving license he glanced at both and looked at the Photos.

I could drive cars, vans and wagons up to 7.5 tonne, the Boss handed me my documents back with a smile on his face and pointed me in the direction of the polish workers. I felt like a sheep running back to its flock for relative safety.

I found the Boss quite intimidating, and I felt that is how he liked it. Once I found the polish workforce, I found myself observing then copying, and generally mucking in wherever I could. We unwrapped cables, changed light bulbs, re-painted equipment and whatever the artists asked us to do without question we did.

Even though the big top was up the circus was definitely not open. It looked like the circus was just coming out of hibernation from the winter months. The artists were perfecting there acts from prancing horses, acrobats, daredevils to clowns they all had their time to practise in the big top. We were making advertising boards for up-and-coming events and according to the boards we were making, we were not due to start our shows for another four weeks in the city of Dusseldorf .

Halfway through my first day everyone stopped working and gathered back outside the boss's caravan and to my surprise the boss's wife, a very classy looking lady with long blond hair and manicured nails, and her daughter came out with platters of crusty bread rolls and not one but two giant pots of meat and potato stew. I couldn't identify the meat, but my empty stomach made no complaints, it was a welcomed boost of energy and the best meal I had had for quite some time. This happened every day to ensure the work force never ran low on much needed energy.

My work colleagues consisted of one Moroccan and six polish men. The Moroccan spoke no English, but he said he could speak German. There was only one problem with that, all he could say in German was "I don't understand". He wasn't much of a conversationalist he was the camel trainer and general dog's body. He had his own trailer to live in which was probably for the best as he did tend to smell like the camels he trained. He seemed to be a happy sole he always had a smile on his face no matter how hard the work got, and he pitched in ware ever help was needed, this man was valued by the boss, hence he was given his own caravan.

One of the polish men said he could speak five different languages English not being one of them. The other Polish were like me still learning German. Other than the obvious communication problems we got on like a house on fire. I learnt you don't have to understand the language to understand the people.

After a hard day's work, the two senior Polish men, the 'Two Andreys' invited me into their wagon and tried to explain everything about the circus, the boss, the pay, the living conditions and a lot more. I had never met two people who complained as much in my life.
 I was to find out that most of these complaints were justified.

The boss was only paying ten Deutsch marks a week, that's the equivalent of 4 English pounds a week. We were getting money for cigarettes and food was provided by the boss's wife that was all. Nobody knew why and to make matters worse the Polish concluded that I could speak better German than them. So, I got nominated to go and talk to the boss about it. I delayed this idea for as long as I could so I could learn more about the circus and learn more German so not to upset the Boss too much.

The old Polish man I had first met couldn't wait and stole one of the circus transit vans as payment. The only problem with that was the circus found him before the police. I wasn't told this till some months later but, the old polish man was seventy-two years of age and the young circus lads found him and gave him a fractured skull and put him in hospital, apparently. I had learnt a valuable lesson never cross the Circus family.

I made two good friends out of the Polish and one night they decided it was time to speak to the boss. So, I got pushed forward to explain what the problem was meaning everyone wants paying. The Boss said he had no money until the circus was on the move in a weeks' time. So, everyone agreed to wait one more week. We also found out how much we would be getting paid, the equivalent of one hundred pounds a week, which I found quite exactable as I was working here for the experience, I came to Europe to see Europe and what better way to do that than travel with a circus.

Yet the Polish people had just come out of communist control to Germany, they were here for one thing and one thing only 'money'. I knew at that time the Polish were not staying, as soon as they got their money they would be leaving.

A week passed and the circus had moved to Dusseldorf but still not opened. Suddenly one of the Polish men walked up to the boss and tried to speak with him the only problem was he was speaking English, what little I had taught him. So, the boss called me over to translate.

Between swear words I managed to translate most of what was said, in short, he said he wouldn't work unless he got paid there and then.

The boss agreed he didn't have to work but if he didn't work, he would have to leave. Then he pointed out that none of us had work papers so none of us had rights. That burst my bubble big style and the reality of the circus life hit me, but I kept quiet. I wanted some money so I could leave the circus and fund my travels, so far, the boss had only given us enough to survive but I was surviving. If I was to leave with no money I might as well have committed suicide because it was still too cold to be out on the streets with no money and no food.

I had already had a taste of hypothermia and I was not in a rush to experience that anytime soon.

In all honesty the boss looked after the workers at the circus like they were family he was responsible for everyone's welfare. When it was quiet and money wasn't coming in the bare essential's food, drink and heating were supplied yet when the good times of plenty came the boss shared what he got, well family look out for each other, and they also suffer together.

This challenge by the polish man was like a slap across the face, and very insulting. I was surprised how reserved the boss was and because of this he earnt my respect.

Two days after this altercation with the Boss, the two Polish men, who I had befriended, came to my wagon to ask a favour, to look after their bags while they looked for work in the city. They weren't staying around any longer.

So, I took their bags to my wagon to keep them safe. Soon after I went to work alone and worked until midnight fixing and preparing circus equipment. With less people in the work force everyone had to work twice as hard, the work was split there was the setting up jobs like, pulling ropes, hitting 5ft tent pegs into the hard ground around the tents, winding ratchet handles, setting the lights and putting the stadium seats together to ensure we were all ready. Once the big top was ready for the show, we all had one day of rest then the shows were to run 2 to 3 shows a day at times for up to two weeks in any one town.

When I returned to my wagon I found my polish friends bags were gone and in their place was a note on top of a carboard box, the note read " Thanks for everything, you are a good friend these are yours" with that I opened the box to see a pair of puma disc system trainers in my size this was a welcomed break for my feet as my boots were looking and feeling a bit worse for ware and this gift gave my feet a well-deserved rest from my heavy boots.

The following morning there was a knock at my door and there stood a giant of a man dressed in a smart suit and waistcoat he must have been in his late 30's early 40's he had dark skin and a welcoming smile he introduced himself as Kaly. I invited him in and offered him a cup of tea, to my surprise he replied "well that's a very English thing to do" in perfect English. He went on to explain that he had dated a English woman for over 4 years so his English was quite good but this wasn't the only language he had mastered, he could speak Italian, French, Spanish, German and his native tongue Moroccan Arabic.

He had worked for the circus before, and he went on the tell me about his brothers who were all part of an acrobatics troop who were all in the USA traveling in a circus over there. I did ask why he had not gone with them, and he told me because of his chequered past he was not allowed into America, so he decided to stay with German Circus as a helping hand till his troops returned.

He asked for the key to the small circus trailer my friends had been living in. After finishing our cups of tea, I helped him to his accommodation feeling much better after at long last meeting my first English speaking person in the circus. After Kaly arrived at the circus it must have been no more than three days then all the polish workers left in the dead of night.

Chapter 9

The Show Must Go ON

On the morning of the Grand opening the atmosphere in the circus ground was electrified everyone seemed to be on tender hooks, to my shock I was handed some black trousers and a sparkly light green jacked to wear while the show was on.

Our jobs then changed to circus ring safety assistants, if someone wanted us to hold a rope, jump into the crowd to extinguish fires that was our job, whatever they told us to do was our job, from showing the customers to their seats to helping stop the wheel of death from spinning and everything in-between.

I can still remember the very first time I worked in the Big Top it was a magical yet terrifying experience but totally worth the poor wages and long hours. The circus brass band played dramatic music to the gathering crowds as they took their seats.

The atmosphere backstage was manic with dogs, goats, camels, dancing girls and prancing horses adorned in sparkling harnesses with millions of sequins reflecting the bright lights.

This Circus didn't have any what you could call dangerous animals as such. But if you have ever met a camel they could be classed as strong minded, stubborn and maybe a little dangerous.

Yet my personal favourite animal just had to be Jock, the star of the show in my eyes he was a little white and tan Shetland pony. Jock was part of a double act little Jock and a massive black stallion by the name of Jet, they were inseparable, and they danced together. Jock would weave in and out of the legs of Jet then Jet would lie down, and Jock would rest his front feet on the mighty stallion.

Once the lights dimmed that told everyone the show was starting, the first person through the curtains was the Boss, the Ring Master.

The other helpers and I found our positions around the edge of the circus ring and waited for instructions from the ring master.

I stood there and I could feel my heart racing as my senses seem to be on high alert. The show started as the band began with the song (love is in the air), the prancing horses and riders entered the arena at a gallop, I could smell and see the shimmering airborne particles of sawdust that had been kicked up into the lights. After the horses, came the clowns then the artists, they had fire breathers, bed of nails, acrobats, magic and specialist acts. There was one man who balanced 18 chairs on top of each other and topped it with a handstand high in the stratosphere of the big top with no safety rope or net.

There was also the wheel of death, which spanned 30 meters across suspended by steel cables on a central spindle like a bike wheel.

At one end was a single circle of steel were up to two artists could stand one on the outside and one on the inside. Then at the other end is were counterbalance weights are placed. So, when you pushed the weights, you could start it spinning sending the artists skywards.

From that day I was circus mad. This madness lasted about two weeks, then I started aching in places I had never ached in my life. Circus work was indeed hard work, but it was also enjoyable at times too.

 I had a go on the wheel of death, while they were training with a safety net, a lot of trust is needed, and a bit of youthful invincibility goes a long way. I only walked around the inside of the wheel of death and that was more than enough to put me off even attempting to walk around the outside of the wheel, like the artist did on a daily basis.

The boss's son, a young lad no more than 16 or 17 years of age performed on this equipment with his grand finale running around the outside of the ring while playing a trumpet at a fast tempo and to make this a truly death-defying performance he did it all blindfolded. Like I said youthful invincibility goes a long way, but this lad had truly nerves of steel.

Over my time with the Circus, I must have seen this act being performed time and time again with not a thing out of place. Then one time he was running around the outer edge as the audience held their breath as he spun round and round at a heart racing speed. His Dad, the ring master and all of us workers were waiting for the hand signal to move in to slow him down, then out of nowhere as the wheel reached its apex he slipped and stumbled forward, the crowd gasped in shock as did his father who watched on helplessly.

Within a split second he somersaulted, removed his blindfold and started to fall, he reached out his hand and grabbed the edge of the circular cage and swung himself back into the relative safety of the inside of the wheel of death just in the nick of time.

In that second everyone rushed to slow and stop the wheel at the top of its cycle. This did give the audience the impression that all what they had witnessed was part of the act, but we knew and more to the point his dad knew, just how close his son had come to be dead or at least seriously injured. Injury is always a possibility in this line of work.

As the polish had left, obviously the circus needed new labourers and they did not advertise these jobs in the jobcentre. Kaly told me that the Moroccan camel trainer had sent for workers from his tribal lands and within just a few days I was introduced to five Berber Moroccan men none of which spoke English or German. Now there is a distinct difference between Kaly and the Berber Moroccans, Kaly was a normal sociable Moroccan.

But these five new workers were Berbers which are tribal Moroccans some may say nomads they spoke a different dialect of Arabic which even Kaly could not understand fully, they are known to be quite territorial, aggressive and of course hard working, perfect for the circus life.

The boss was aware of the characteristics of these men, so all the Berbers were accommodated in their own long trailer. This trailer was about 18 ft long and had four single doors along its side. At the side of the trailer each door opened to a small room with a bunk bed and a small sink, a very compact place to live but Berbers travelled light, a few clothes, personal items and a prayer mat as they were practising Muslims.

The first morning the Berbers started work I was woken by the sound of what I thought to be a jackhammer a pneumatic jackhammer bang, bang, bang, bang in quick succession again and again.

I opened the door to investigate, to my astonishment four of the Berber workers were stood around a 5 ft tent peg all holding a ten-pound lump hammer. They tapped it into the ground, so it stood level, then one after another they swung back to strike the peg in sequence and in rhythm with each other. As one hammer head hit the peg the other hammer head was on its way down one after the other until the 5 ft steal pegs were sunk into the frost covered ground what would take me, or Kaly a good 15 minutes took them no more than 2 minutes.

The good news was the workforce was as strong as ever and the erection of the big top was a lot easier with the Berbers and completed in half the time. When the circus was on the move, I was responsible for driving a van towing the snack trailer. On one occasion after stopping for the toilet I got myself lost and I turned up to the new circus ground 2 hours late. Kaly told me that the Boss was starting to think I had run away with his equipment and was in the process of putting together a group to come and find me. From that day I was never late as I feared that I might share the same fate as the old polish man. We travelled all around Germany for a few months then we packed up after our last evening show in Germany then the Circus headed for Holland.

Chapter 10

Deadly Consequences

In Holland

Our first stop in Holland was in a city called Eindhoven we travelled through the night and arrived in the early hours everyone was exhausted and relieved that the Boss had decided that we could have Two days break before setting up the big top for our first Show. I had my time off all planned I intended to get cleaned up and head out to find a Night club to experience being a normal 22-yearold just for one Night. I had managed to save nearly 200 Deutsch Marks and I felt I deserved one night of normality. Although first above anything else I needed sleep, I slept till 1 O'clock the following afternoon.

After lighting the kindling in the log burner, I heated the water and had a good standing wash and shave using a torn rag, some shower gel and an old Bic razor I found at the bottom of my rucksack.

After putting on my best, cleanest clothes and for that moment I felt like a normal human once more. Just as I was lacing up my shoes there was a knock at the door it was Kaly, and he wasn't alone. To my shock he had the Boss and the camel trainer with him, my initial thought was (what have I done now). As I spent a lot of my down time in the animal tents helping and feeding Jock the Shetland pony the odd apple.

The Boss looked very concerned, and he asked Kaly to interpret from German to English to ensure I understood. Kaly went on to explain that the Camel Trainer needed medical treatment because of an injury to his hand I glanced over to the trainer, and he had his right hand wrapped in a dirty stained cloth and he was cradling this hand with his good left hand the constant smile I had got to know so well was gone.

I was a bit confused to what they expected me to do so Kaly went on to explain that this Moroccan man had no medical insurance so he could not get any medical help and as he was technically an illegal work a black worker, a worker with no papers, this complicated the matter further. Now British Citizens could get treatment anywhere in the world on a form called a E111 a health insurance form and as part of my preparation for my trip I had a E111 form with me. But this poor man had no such safety net.

As he needed immediate medical advice and it seemed up to 70% of the people in Holland spoke English. The Boss asked me if I could go with him to a local doctor and if need be, use my medical insurance to get this man treated. I agreed to help and grabbed my jacket. We sat the camel trainer in the back of the Bosses new shiny Mercedes-Benz then I took my seat up front with the Boss and we set off.

Kaly stayed behind so I was back to the little germen I had learnt.

Shortly after we set off the Boss pointed at the glove compartment and said, "money in there". With that I opened the glove compartment to see not only the biggest wad of banknotes I had ever seen but laying on top of this money was a

 Browning nine-millimetre pistol with its magazine clearly located in the pistol grip, to anyone who has spent time in the British armed force this firearm is commonplace and very distinctive as an officer's side arm. I was aware that the Boss was watching me and looking for a reaction but aside from the initial intake of breath when I saw this pistol, I quickly regained my composure and calmly lifted the pistol up just enough to slide the cash out from beneath it and within that second, I could tell by the weight of this firearm this pistol was loaded with a full mag.

I passed the boss his money and after he flicked through the wad, he passed me back a few hundred Dutch Gilden for any costs if needed at the doctors.

It seemed to take hours to get to the doctor's surgery even though in reality it must have been no more than 20 minutes or so. As we pulled into the car park the boss pointed towards the reception.

With the cash tightly grasped in my sweaty hand I helped the camel trainer from the Boss's car, and the Boss made it clear that he had no intention of coming in with us.

Obviously, the camel trainer looked very concerned and confused, well if I were in a strange country where I didn't understand the culture, or the languages spoken around me and knowing that everything what was said was about me I think I would be worried just as much as this poor man. We walked through the automatic doors to be hit by a warm jet of air coming from the heated waiting area.

I was relieved that the receptionist spoke English quite well and she explained that this was a drop-in clinic, so I gave her my details and my E111 form and she asked us to wait to be called by the Doctor.

Our turn came quickly, and we were sat in front of the doctor a slim elderly man with pale face, who also spoke very good English. I went on to explain that this dark-skinned Moroccan was Robert Winter and he needed medical attention.

The Doctor promptly replied in perfect English "Now would you like to tell me the truth". He went on to explain that he was educated in Oxford University, and he was not stupid, he also explained that whoever needs medical assistance he was duty bound to give treatment or advice too regardless of their race or ability to pay.

I apologised for trying to mislead him and explained that the camel trainer needed his help.

The Doctor started the examination he removed the dirty rag that was wrapped around his hand and the room filled with a pungent smell like a cross between rotting eggs and meat mixed, the smell made my eyes water and the back of my throat burn.

After the Doctor had opened the window then cleaned the wound and placed a fresh dressing on the wound, he turned to me and asked if the camel trainer understood any Dutch or English I replied, "No he just understood a little German".

So, the Doctor went on to tell me that it wasn't good news, my work colleague had advanced gangrene in his finger and that he needed immediate treatment to save his life.

Which left me with the unfortunate task of explaining to the camel trainer of this news and the treatment the doctor said would be lifesaving, in what little germen I could speak and obviously in the simplest way so he could understand the severity of his predicament.

So as the Doctor spoke to me in English I communicated to the camel trainer by broken German, facial expressions and hand gestures and I tried to get this unfortunate soul to understand his medical situation. The Doctor said "the gangrene had spread though his finger and passed his knuckle so the only treatment to save his life would be to amputate his right hand and start him on strong antibiotics to stop the infection traveling further, any delay would mean he would lose his arm or indeed his life from blood poisoning. After I had processed what I had heard with tears in my eyes I explained this to the best of my ability.

By his immediate response I was sure he had understood the procedure which was needed to save his life.

The camel Trainer became very protective over his hand and when the doctor handed him some strong antibiotics, he snatched them from his hand and walked out of the building determined that nobody was chopping his hand off.

I tried to explain to the boss on the way back to the circus ground but we both decided to wait until Kaly was with us, so everybody knew what had been said and understood the severity of the situation.

To my relief as we pulled up at the Circus Kaly appeared from the boss's caravan, so I went on to explain in English to Kaly the diagnosis and more importantly the prognosis the doctor had given.

Kaly thanked me for trying to help his Moroccan colleague, and now he knew all the details. The Boss told me to grab something to eat and he would take things from here and Kaly would update me later as Kaly sat down with the boss and the camel trainer to discuss what they were to do from there. So, I returned to my trailer with my thoughts and sympathy for this poor soul.

It seemed a lot longer than it was but true to his word Kaly came to update me on what had been decided.

The camel trainer had decided to return to Morocco and not seek treatment, but to return to his country to die. I thought Kaly had not understood me that if he had his hand amputated, he could live. But this was understood and taken into consideration. Kaly went on to explain that to have your hand cut off in Morocco was a sign that you have been caught stealing and it brought dishonour to your family. So, he would be shunned by his tribe if he had his hand cut off, he could not live with this shame, so he had decided to put his fate in Allah's hands, as a devote Muslim. To me this seemed brutal and unfair for this man who always had a smile for everyone no matter how hard the work got. but I had to respect this person's beliefs and wishes.

After Kaly left, I decided to go to a local bar to drink a toast to the camel trainer. I no longer was in the mood for a nightclub. Nobody knows what may be around the corner.

Chapter 11

New Day New Challenges

The following morning came with a clear sky and a heavy heart, I was still in shock over what had transpired the day before. I was hoping the doctor had been wrong or the camel trainer had decided to seek treatment but neither had happened.

 I met up with Kaly and the workforce as normal and Kaly told me that the camel trainer had started his journey back to Morocco and his mind had been made up to die in his own country around his own people with his families honour still intact.

The youngest and smallest of the Berber Moroccan worked with the Camel trainer so he took on the duties in his absence. That day a lot of things became apparent; everyone was feeling down regarding the camel trainer the atmosphere in camp was a solemn one and every time I was around the Berber Moroccans, I got the distinct impression that they held me at least partially responsible for their fellow Moroccan's fate it wasn't a welcoming atmosphere like before.

A few days later I was called to the Bosses caravan, he explained that my duties were to change as he had employed two young Dutch men in their 20s to promote the circus while in Holland and he wanted me to work alongside them, traveling ahead of the main circus to put up posters and hand out flyers.

The Dutch men were called Daan and Dirk, they were living in a small caravan the boss had got just for the time they were working with us. They were very well looked after and they only worked with each other, doing all the preparation work regarding the posters and flyers, they didn't have to do any other work.
 But me on the other hand, I still had to perform my normal duties, putting the big top up, assembling the seating & working in the arena when the show was on. Once the Dutch lads had finished their preparation work and loaded their van with all the advertising posters and banners, only then my duties were to change.

I would get a break for a few days helping Daan & Dirk put up posters and hand out flyers so at least I had a brief break from the normal circus work I had got accustomed to.

Daan and Dirk were typical 21-year-old Dutch men, they could speak a host of languages. There main interests were making money and just as fast spending it on beer, marijuana and the pursuit of women, now they could drink like fish and smoke like chimneys.
Though their success rate in the pursuit of women was, well a bit hit and miss at the best of times. But they were happy and friendly to all. I had many entertaining nights drinking and smoking till the early hours to regret it the very next morning when I had to start work while they got the chance to sleep off their hangovers, I was not so lucky.

One night after getting my wage I finished work and I had arranged to meet up with Dann and Dirk at a local Night club, they had told me to jump in a taxi as there was only one club in the area.

I had it all planned, get out of my sparkling jacket, have a quick wash then find myself a taxi. In quick time I was in the taxi on my way to what I believed to be my first good night out since getting to the circus.

The taxi seemed to be going past the town centre, so I asked the driver "are you going to a night club" in which he replied "yes the best night club in the area" with a smile on his face from ear to ear, I sat back and waited. It wasn't long till the taxi driver pulled down a poorly lit street and said in a cheerful voice "we are here".

As I looked out the window all I could see was a dark quiet alleyway, with very little going on.

At first, I though the driver was trying to rip me off. But then the driver just pointed at a black door with a small hatch in it and said "Night club have fun" so I paid the driver and approached this strange doorway not knowing what to expect while the taxi driver watched on. As I got closer to the door to my relief I could hear faint dance music coming from the other side, so I knocked on the hatch and stood back.

Within seconds the hatch slid open to reveal a large, coloured man, I immediately asked "is this the night club" to which his responded "yes" while he looked me up and down. Suddenly the hatch slammed shut then to my relief the door swung open to welcome me in.

As soon as I walked in, I noticed that the music wasn't that loud and in front of me was a dimly lit bar, without any further delay I made my way to the bar and asked for a large beer, as I waited for my drink, I started to look around to see if I could see my friends. I couldn't see them anywhere.

As I looked down the bar all I could see was couples sat along the bar, all the men seemed to be smartly dressed in shirts and ties. Then my attention was brought to the ladies sat next to them, who were all stunning and more noticeable was they were all wearing very sexy lingerie, all of them in stockings and suspenders.

With this I turned to the barman who had just placed my beer in front of me and asked again "is this NOT a night club"? Before he could answer me, a door opened behind me then one beautiful lady after another came out in single file until I had a whole collection of sexy ladies stood there in front of me, all in high heels and sexy outfits.

I turned back to the barman when he asked me "are you English" after nodding my head, whilst not trying to give anyone eye contact, he said I think you are looking for a disco tech not a night club.

The barman went on to explain that in holland a disco tech is an English night club and obviously, a night club in holland was a gentleman's club in England. To my relief the barman took this misunderstanding in good humour, but I cannot say the same for the ladies, as the barman explained to the ladies of the misunderstanding, I must have heard abusive language in over 10 different languages all directed at me, as they all walked back behind the door to wait for their next customer.

 While I was finishing my beer and waiting for my taxi, I did ask the barman just out of interest, how much does it cost and how does it all work he told me if I had to ask, I could probably not afford the service, and the girls always order champagne.

 With my night drawing to a close I jumped in my taxi and I returned back to the circus to dream of the delights that I could not afford.

After a few weeks working alongside my Dutch counterparts, I was called to the Bosses caravan once more, the boss explained that the Berber Moroccans had complained to him, and they felt that the boss was showing favouritism over me. I had my own caravan with a wood burning stove and they all shared one long caravan segmented into two bed compartments. So, the boss asked me to move my things into one of the compartments in the Berbers caravan to try and show that there was no favouritism and subdue the Berber workforce.

I think the Berber which complained expected the boss to move him into my accommodation and me into his, but the boss didn't think like that, and I got moved into the same compartment as the Moroccan who had made the complaint which was just as much of a shock to me, as it was to him.

It became obvious that I was not welcome and that the Berbers had decided they didn't want me out of the single caravan anymore, they wanted me out of the circus .As the Moroccan man was sat on the bottom bunk of the bunkbed in this very small space, I threw my things on the top bunk rolled out my sleeping bag and organised my things then I went on with my day, leaving this very confused and upset Berber sat probably wishing he had not said anything to the boss.

After a hard day's work, I returned to my new accommodation, half expecting my things to be missing but everything was where I had left it. After I grabbed myself something to eat, I got myself comfortable on the top bunk it was not long before my roommate returned from his work. He was banging and clattering about a lot. He eventually got himself settled on his bunk under me, to my relief. Then all I could hear was a scrapping sound coming from the bottom bunk, scrape, scrape, scrape this went on for quite some time, so I glanced over the edge to see what he was up to.

To my surprise my roommate was sat up with a head torch on holding a little one-inch penknife, sharpening to a point, what seemed to be a snapped piece of wood off a mop handle.

No matter how hard I tried to think of a none menacing reason why he was sharpening this sturdy piece of wood to a point.
I could only think "this was for me", as you would except, I didn't get much sleep that night.

The next morning after having very little to no sleep I heard my roommate stir and start moving around, as I glanced to the door, I saw him grab his prayer mat and head off to join the other Berbers for morning prayers. Without hesitation I jumped down from my bunk to see what my Moroccan roommate had been making, I lifted his pillow and there tucked under his bed sheets were, not one, but two five-inch hand crafted wooden stakes with string bound handle grips the workmanship was quite outstanding but the intention of these items were of course very concerning.

These items were not tools they were obviously weapons. I sat on the floor of the caravan with the wooden stakes in my hands as I waited for my roommate to return. I could hear his steps as he made his way to the door, as it swung open, we came face to face I jumped to my feet and shouted, "what the hell are these for?". with that the startled Moroccan stumbled and fell backwards on the dry earth outside the caravan, as he laid there with a shocked expression on his face I jumped down from the caravan and repeated "what the hell are these for? ". At that moment one of the artists came from around the corner, grabbed hold of both of us and told us that if we had a problem we were to go to the boss. I said I had a problem alright "This Berber is crazy and he's planning to kill me" I then explained to the artist what had happened. With that the artist took us both to see the boss.

There we stood like naughty school children expecting no less than the cane. That must have been the most demoralising situation I had ever been faced with. The boss was stood in front of me waiting for an explanation. I told him what had happened with the Berber. I was glad to find the boss had the same attitude to fighting with weapons as I did. He pushed me to one side and with one almighty swing of his arm he knocked the Berber clean off his feet. Then he turned to me and said,

"No more trouble with Berbers is that clear?"

To my relief he also moved me back to a wagon of my own away from all the Berbers. I agreed there would be no more trouble on my behalf. The Berber didn't get a second chance he was banished from the circus that day.

Normally there is no fighting amongst the circus people and if there was to be any violence it was to come from the boss. Everybody obeyed that rule, and I came close to stepping over that line.

Once I was back in my old accommodation, everything seemed to get back to normal and settle down, then out of the blue whilst me and Kaly were working, moving equipment around and getting ready for the next show in the preparation area of the big top. As I bent down to move a small table, I felt a sudden gust of wind whistle around my ear followed by a sudden thud sound, with that I turned to see Kaly's hand right next to my ear, his hand was clenched around a large steel bar. My eyes followed the shaft of the bar and there at the other end was the small Berber Moroccan with a very angry expression on his face it was clear this man intended to kill me.

He seemed to hold me responsible for the camel trainer's fate and his colleague being kicked out..

At that moment seeing the hatred in his eyes, I was overcome with anger. I jumped towards my assailant knocked the bar out of his hand, swept his feet away from under him then I jumped on top of him.

Then with my fists tightly clenched, I focused all my punches at his head not to give him the opportunity to strike with whatever weapons he may have had concealed on him. Time seemed to slow down even though this lasted only seconds it felt like minutes.

Then I was lifted into the air and thrown a good 10 meters. I jumped to my feet excepting to be faced with more Berbers but no there stood shadowing over me was the Boss.

He moved towards me shouting "so you want to fight, I'm the only one who fights in my Circus". Before I could say anything, Kaly stepped between us and explained that I was only defending myself and that the small Berber swung an iron bar at my head.

If Kaly hadn't seen the bar and acted when he did, I would have surely died that day.

Once Kaly had explained to the Boss what had gone on the Boss turned to me and told me to go back to my trailer. Without wanting to aggravate him any more than I had already I quickly left the big top leaving the Boss and circus lads to decide the fate of the small Berber.

It didn't come as a surprise when Kaly told me that the small Berber had been kicked out of the Circus and he also told me that I had to keep my head down as the Boss was still upset at me regardless of if I was acting in self-defence or not.

It's a whole new ball game, circus life, after this I focused on staying out of the Bosses way and saving as much money as possible, so I had the funds to leave. After a month of hard graft and saving as much as I could the time came to move on. I had to remind myself why I was in Europe, to travel and to meet people but to make money as well. I found myself travelling and meeting people but with very little money. That was the downfall of the circus, they would pay enough money to buy food, cigarettes and a little beer but not enough to leave.

As I was a driver the boss classed me as a valuable commodity. It would have been unwise to tell him I was leaving. I knew if I were caught leaving, I could end up in hospital. So, I only told three very good friends whom I knew I could trust when I wanted to leave. The only people who knew was Kaly of course and Daan and Dirk who joined the circus in Holland. I needed their help to get away because they were the forward party for the next town. That night I bundled my bag into the back of their van and I was driven away under cover of darkness.

The people who helped me weren't just putting their jobs on the line they were putting their health on the line as well. It takes real friends to do that. Halfway between the two towns I decided to leave my friend's company, so I said my goodbyes to my new friends, relieved that my time in the circus had come to an end and I was still in one piece.

I suppose everyone does crazy things from time to time and so far, it had been a totally crazy journey.

For the first time in a long time, I was in no hurry to do anything, I had time on my hands, and I had saved some money from the circus so where to next.

I had heard about the south of France only in books and from other people's recollections. It's nice to hear other people's recollections but it's even better to have your own memories. I think that must be the reason I decided to make my way to France also I had heard that there was quite a lot of seasonal workers, fruit pickers needed. But first I took a few days of doing very little but resting in my tent and exploring the local area. I came across a small village store just a few miles from where I had made camp, so I stocked up on pot noodles, water, bread, some well-deserved razors and a notebook to start jotting down my travels so far.

After a few days just resting in my trusted tent, I had forged a plan.

Chapter 12
The New Plans New Direction

As I found myself near the border of Belgium, indicated by a nearby signpost for Antwerp and the small border town of Tilburg which was only 8km up the road. My plan was to hitchhike down to Bordeaux France a renowned area for its wine and vineyards. This seemed to be a good place to start after studying the road network in my European road Atlas. I decided to stick to the main roads and motorway routes, even though this would be a much longer route in distance I would stand more chance of being picked up on the main routes. I planned to move across Belgium through East Flanders to then cross over into France near the border town of Mouscron. I had planned to avoid big cities where I could, but I would still need to navigate Antwerp ring road to get onto the A14 which would take me to the boarder of France. This would complete the first stage of my journey.

I figured that this route would be just under 200 km, in a car about 2 ½ hours' drive but by my thumb who knows.

The sun was shining, and my tent was dry, I felt recharged, all my equipment was clean and packed away. On top of it all I felt human again after a wash and shave which was well overdue. These few days of rest in a field in Holland was just what was needed. With high spirits and no schedule, I started the first leg towards Bordeaux.

As I was walking following the signposts for Antwerp with the sun on my back, listening to the morning chorus of the bird songs all around. I noticed in the distance a shadow, like a cloud, but this cloud was moving, moving fast towards me. As the cloud got closer over the flat expanse of agricultural land around me, it became clear that this shadowing cloud consisted of over 1000 awe-inspiring Starlings performing like a synchronised aerial display team, as they approached, they changed direction in unison without a sound.

They seemed to be dancing around me, they circled me 3- or 4-times changing direction time and time again. As I was mesmerised with this acrobatic display, I failed to notice a car had stopped just feet away from me. With a beep of the cars horn my attention was brought away from this hypnotic display, and I found myself looking at the car that had stopped next to me, and what a car this was.

There in front of me was a top of the range Mercedes – Benz Coupe, not with one burbling exhaust pipe but four. It looked like a missile all in stunning gun metal silver complete with aerodynamic lines running down the full length of this automotive masterpiece.
This was not the type of car I would have expected to stop for a hitchhiker.
The driver jumped out and asked in German if I wanted to put my backpack in the boot and to jump in. Without hesitation I replied, "yes please", also in German.

With that we loaded the car and pulled way.
 Now the driver was a smartly dressed man in his late 40s early 50s he looked like your typical businessman and his name was Otto and to my relief he also spoke English. After chatting for a while, it became apparent that Otto was an automotive engineer and he worked as a freelance specialist for Mercedes, it seemed that Otto was at the top of his game.

Otto asked where I was heading so I told him my plan, it turned out that Otto was on his way to Antwerp, and he offered to drop me at the far side of the city to help me with my ongoing travel. With that I settled into the plush surroundings of this amazing car all the way to the A14 at the far side of Antwerp. Time seemed to pass extremely fast, we talked about Otto's work and my travels and of course cars. It turned out that Otto had Hitchhiked in his youth so whenever he could, he would always stop for hitchhikers (a true kindred spirit). As we pulled up at the first main exit off the A14, near a town called St-Niklaas this is where we were to part ways.

I thanked Otto for his generosity, and he helped me unload my backpack, wished me luck and he went on his way with a burble of his exhausts pipes he disappeared into the distance. I couldn't believe my luck.

Where I had been dropped looked much like where Otto had picked me up. I was nearly halfway through my first leg to Bordeaux, and it wasn't even midday. With luck on my side I decided to find a quiet place to brew up from my supplies before commencing my onward travel.

Belgium seemed to be a very clean country mainly agricultural and extremely flat, coming from the Yorkshire Dales this landscape did feel quite alien to me, I never thought you could miss hills, but I did.

After packing my stove and mug I got back to the roadside to see what fate had in store for me.

I was in good health and good spirits so with a spring in my step and my thumb stretched out I waited for my next lift and then I waited some more.

The wind started to pick up and storm clouds started to gather. Then within seconds I heard a distance crack of thunder then the rain came, it seemed within twenty minutes it went form clear skies to a torrential downpour with thunder and lightning creeping closer and closer. As I was stood at the roadside it quickly became apparent that apart from the passing wagons, I was the tallest object along this stretch of road. The road was raised above the fields and farmland to reduce the effects of flooding with embankments down to the fields on both sides I was the tallest target for the incoming lightning. Not wishing to become a human lightning conductor, I made my way down the embankment to a farm track which passed under the road where I had been stood, to take cover from the ensuing storm.

As I got to the opening of the underpass an almighty crack of thunder echoed all around me followed by a blue flash of lightning which shimmered off the droplets streaming down from the road above. I wasn't sure where the lightning had hit but I could feel and smell the electrical static in the air all around me. After my senses returned, I found myself standing with mud up to my ankles, soaked from head to toe.

I was left dazed, confused and quite scared of how close I was to this awesome natural power, above all I felt small and very insignificant in this storm. The feeling of safety didn't return until the storm had past some hours later. At the end of this ordeal, I felt emotionally and physically exhausted, once I was sure the storm had passed, I made my way into a field just off the track to set up camp and get out of my drenched and cold clothes. Once I had discarded my wet clothes and got comfortable in my sleeping bag I dozed off for a much-needed night's sleep.

Chapter 13
Unexpected Detour

The next morning, I awoke to an engine noise in the distance getting seemingly quieter as the sound faded into the atmosphere. I thought nothing of it until I felt a cold breeze and noticed the door of the tent flapping in the wind. My wet clothes I had placed at the doorway had been moved and my lightweight jacket was gone, then it occurred to me that I had been robbed.

In a frenzy I checked all my belongings to find that most of the money I had managed to save while working in the circus was gone, even more worrying was my passport was also gone. My situation was back to a bit of food and what little money I had in my trouser pockets. My stomach churned as the realisation of my predicament became clear, it was time to reassess my situation as going to France didn't seem to be an option anymore.

I must have sat there assessing what my options were for a good 15 minutes, my emotions flickered from anger to despair and back again. I found myself hyperventilating and then I shut my eyes and started to control my breathing I told myself, breath in, breath out repeatedly then eventually I regained my composure to allow my mind the chance to grasp a more helpful thought pattern. I grabbed my road atlas and assessed my options go North over 100 miles to the ferry ports of Dieppe or Rotterdam and hope help would be there or retrace my footsteps back to the Border of Holland which was a lot closer.

My first concern had to be getting a replacement passport.
As I was in Belgium, and I couldn't speak or understand the Belgium language it made more sense to retrace my footsteps back to the Dutch border were more people spoke English and communicating would be a lot easier.

With my tent packed away, I set off hoping for a change in my fortune. I must have walked no more than a mile when an old rusty work van stopped in front of me in a cloud of exhaust smoke. I wasn't sure if he had just broken down or had stopped to give me a lift. As the smoke cleared from around this van, I was faced with two smiling faces the younger of the two men opened the passenger door and moved himself into the middle seat to make room for me and my belongings.

Without hesitating I jumped in and thanked them for stopping. With that the younger man said in a strong Yorkshire accent "your English". I asked where in Yorkshire he was from and to my surprise he replied I'm from holland I've never been to England or Yorkshire.

As his accent was stronger than mine, I found it hard to believe that he wasn't even English but Dutch.

I asked where he learnt English and he told me that he watches a lot of English TV and his favourite programs were Emmerdale Farm and Coronation Street, two well-known Northern English TV soaps. I was amazed on just how good his English was just by watching TV.

He went on to explain that he was out working with his Father and that they were stone masons on their way back from looking at a job.

His Father could not speak any English, but his son introduced himself as Steven. I explained to Steven my predicament that I needed to go to a police station in Holland to report my missing passport and get a replacement. Steven picked up a road Atlas off the dashboard to show me exactly where he could drop me. Like many times before these people went out of their way to help and dropped me at the front doors of the first police station they could find.

He offered to come in with me, but I did not wish to delay them anymore than I had already.

I thanked these kind souls and said goodbye, as they left me in a cloud of exhaust fumes. With my eyes slightly watering I put on my backpack and turned to report my misfortune to the Dutch police.

The police station looked much like the ones in the UK, except everyone seemed to be carrying a firearm. After speaking to the Officer at reception, she offered me a coffee then told me to take a seat and wait while they investigated what I would need to do next, as they didn't get many English citizens in my predicament to deal with in their normal day to day duties.

It wasn't long at all until the officer returned with a piece of paper in her hand and a smile on her face, this looked promising. She went on to explain that she had spoken to the British Consulate, she had the address of the office that issued replacement passports under circumstances like my own. It seemed help was just around the corner, she passed me the paper and said they can help in a cheerful reassuring voice. As I read the address it became apparent that help was there, but it was most definitely not just around the corner. The address read British Consulate, 29 Panormastraze, Stuttgart, Germany. Which happened to be 400 + miles away.

I quickly concluded that I needed help, so I asked the officer if I could use their phone to make a call. The call I never wanted to have to make to my father, to ask if he could lend me some money so I could get to Stuttgart and get a replacement passport.

After explaining my situation to my Farther, I asked if he could lend me some money to help, reassuring him I would pay him back as soon as I found my next work. He replied that he would send me £100 with one condition. This condition was, once I got my passport I would come back home to work in the factory and be more responsible. As he always saw this venture as a mistake not as I saw it, as an adventure. I begrudgingly agreed to his terms and the money was sent over.

Chapter 14
The Helping Hand

As I wished to save this money for essentials, I decided to hitchhike to the German border then look at buying a cheap rail ticket to Stuttgart. With that I made my way to the motorway to start my journey.

Based on my journey so far since leaving the circus, I expected very little luck and that seemed to be the case. I was stood at the edge of a roundabout leading to a motorway for at least an hour before the torrential rain came once more but I was grateful that this time there was no thunder just streaming water. I looked around for cover, but the visibility was very poor with the spray from the passing traffic and the down pour bouncing off the tarmac all around me. So, I put the hood up on my waterproof poncho, a piece of equipment I was relieved to have with me, and I just stood there with my legs gradually becoming wetter and colder with each passing vehicle.

Time seemed to pass in slow motion and the sound of the rain drowned out the sound of the traffic, so I retreated into my own little dream world. I started thinking of a warm place with an open fire with logs crackling as they gave off there warming glow. I had completely given up on the prospect of a lift, although I was strangely content in my imaginary world as it seemed so real, yet I knew it was just my mind playing tricks on me, so I could endure the situation I had found myself in.

In the distance I could hear a faint voice saying "hello, hello", I wasn't sure if it was real or still a figment of my imagination. As I lifted my head, I saw red brake lights followed by a bright white reversing light from a large van which was now reversing towards me. Within seconds I was at the side door of this van, the driver jumped over to the sliding side door then slid it open to offer his hand, with a smile on his face. I grabbed his outstretched hand, and he pulled me into the dry warm shelter of his van.

This friendly traveller said something in Dutch as he jumped back into the driving seat. I immediately reply with "I'm sorry I am English", he smiled once more and said, "no need to apologise for being English." as he pulled away with the windscreen wipers going at full speed.

Once I took off my poncho and placed my slightly dripping rucksack on the floor of the van, I jumped over to the passenger seat to join my new temporary traveling companion. It turned out that he was called John he must have been in his late forties, he was delivering some machine parts. Once I had got myself comfortable, with the air vents drying out my trousers. John asked me "so where are you going friend" with a smile on my face I told John "Germany anywhere in Germany". John replied, "not in this van you're not".
It seems I had been hitchhiking on the wrong side of the motorway and with every passing second, I was getting further and further away from Germany.

I apologised to John for any inconvenience and asked if he could drop me off at the next junction to get myself going back in the right direction. After looking out of the window and seeing the rain was just as bad as it was before, John came up with a counter proposal. He needed to get the parts delivered and then he would be coming straight back to the same junction he had picked me up from and hopefully once we had returned the rain would have stopped. I wouldn't have got any closer to Germany but the possibility of continuing my journey dry and recharged was the best idea I had heard for quite some time. With that we continued on our way with the heaters on full blast.

John seemed to be a quite pleasant fellow we talked about the circus and my desire to work around Europe. Then on the way back John told me about his travels in his youth. He had travelled to Australia and India while he was having a year out from his studies. In what seemed to be no time at all we had arrived back where I had started earlier that day and unfortunately the rain was still there as if it was waiting for me.

I thought if I didn't have bad luck, I would have had no luck at all. But the positives where I was dry, refreshed and I had had an enjoyable four hours with John. With that I thanked John and went to grab my bag from the back of the van. John said I could not start hitchhiking in this weather and he offered to take me back to his home.

At this I was quite cautious as I knew very little about John and I had already had the misfortune of meeting a weirdo before. And the thought of going to a stranger's home, gave me cause for concern. Not wishing to tar everyone with the same brush and not wanting to insult John, I asked " can I ask are you a weirdo?," he looked at me quite bemused so I explained that I had to defend myself against someone who had picked me up and I would love to sleep in a nice warm home but I needed to make sure he wasn't a weirdo, or that he expected anything for this favour.

John's look of bemusement turned to shock of what I had told him, and he assured me that I would be safe in his company, he was inviting me to stay at his family's home were his wife and his two younger children lived.

He went on to explain that his eldest son was backpacking around Asia and if his son was in the same situation as I found myself in, he hoped that someone would help him like he wanted to help me. I apologised for asking the questions and he said he wasn't offended it was right to say something, as you never know.

With the air cleared we made are way to John's home for the night, on the outskirts of the city of Maastricht.

We arrived at Johns at just gone 6 O'clock after a full day of travelling. John lived in a ground floor flat in a small block, it seemed like a quiet and clean area. As we got to the front door it swung open and two small children rushed out and threw their arms around their dad's neck.

John with one child in each arm, introduced me to his two younger children, his 7-year-old son Lucas and his 6-year-old daughter Eline. These youngsters must have been the most pleasant children I had ever had the pleasure to meet. You could tell they had been raised by a loving family.

Even though they were so young there manners just like there English were faultless. I felt welcome even before I had stepped through the doorway. Then their mother called the children from the kitchen and told them to get ready for bed while she made them some hot chocolate. John introduced me to his wife, Saskia. She was a petite lady in her mid to late 40s and she was obviously devoted to her family. John's flat consisted of a large open plan living room which led onto a kitchen, off the living room there were doors that led to three bedrooms and a bathroom, it was decorated with family photos and artwork which the children had done.

Johns' wife had already laid out a towel and a change of clothes for john and as John had already phoned his wife, she had also laid out a second towel for me. The kindness of this family seemed to have touched my very soul.

After John had a shower, I followed and changed into some clean clothes I had safely packed in my bag. To sit down in this warm family environment was just what I needed, the atmosphere seemed to wash all my stresses away. Lucas and Eline wanted to know everything, where I had come from, where I had been and where I was going. Their interests seemed to be magnified as their older brother had set off on his own travels only weeks before. They even asked if I had met him on my travels.

After the children had finished their questions and hot chocolate, their mum told them to say goodnight and make their way into their bedroom so they could read for a while before lights out.

With that they hugged their dad and said goodnight as their mum walked them to their bedroom. When Saskia came back into the living room, she had her arms full of crisp fresh bedding and fluffy pillows, which she placed next to me on the sofa I couldn't thank her enough.

After the kids were put to bed, we sat eating pizza which Saskia had prepared.

Whilst chatting in this relaxing atmosphere, I was asked what my plans were regarding getting to Stuttgart and John insisted that he would take me to the train station the next morning as it was Saturday, and he did not work at weekends. Soon after they left me to get comfortable on their sofa and retired to their bedroom. I could hear the children talking amongst themselves in their native tongue. It sounded like they were too excited to sleep.

But I wasn't the only one to overhear them as Saskia crept through the living room to try and quieten the youngsters, not wishing them to disturb me.

I glanced over to their room to see Saskia tucking Lucus and Eline into their bunkbeds, then she gave them each a kiss on the cheek and said goodnight, a truly loving family.

Saskia noticed that I was awake she picked up a nearby blanket and draped it over me then she knelt, kissed my forehead and whispered goodnight, sweet dreams with a kind and reassuring smile. I drifted off to sleep, with a tear in my eye from the kindness I had been shown, I truly felt their love, like I was at home.

Not so early the next morning I opened my eyes to the sight of two cheerful faces staring back at me as the children announced to their mother that "Rob was awake!"

It seemed that they were told to keep quiet, and they were not allowed to watch cartoons on the TV until Rob had woken. A true dilemma for any child indeed.

Saskia asked me if they had disturbed me and of course I said they had not, so the Cartoons began, Popeye the sailor man in Dutch. After watching as a child the same cartoons, but in English, this mesmerised me.

John had gone to a nearby shop for some milk and Saskia was in the process of making breakfast, the smell was amazing, a sweet Aromatic smell was coming from the kitchen with a hint of ginger in the air. She was preparing a breakfast I later found to be called Groninger koek it was a warm Dark brown loaf which she cut into slices and smothered each slice in butter. Once John had returned, she passed around plates with two slices each and we all had fruit juice and coffee.

Once we had finished, I packed away my belongings and turned to say my goodbyes to this loveable family unit.

Lucus and Eline gave me a hug and asked me to keep a look out for their big brother. Saskia handed me a packed lunch to take on my way, and with a small peck on the cheek and a smile, she bid me farewell. I couldn't thank John enough for he didn't just give me a place to stay for the night he did much more, he put my faith back in humanity.

From a distance the Maastricht Railway station looked more like a town hall or a private school than a railway station, with a big red brick clock tower dominating the righthand side of the skyline. After saying farewell to my generous host, I made my way in to find a ticket office to see just how much a ticket to Germany would be. As I walked through the front door the beauty of the architecture astounded me; the room opened to a cathedral type ceiling curved high above my head. I walked to the middle of this grand hall to suddenly be surrounded by vivid colours all around me on the floor.

I then turned back to the doorway I had entered by to be faced with the morning sun beaming through the stained-glass windows above the entrance, all depicting saints and shields and all redirecting these vibrant colours of light.

I was relieved to find the ticket office and an English-speaking assistant, I explained that I was needing to get to Germany in the cheapest manor to then make my way to Stuttgart. I was told that the cheapest route would be to Düsseldorf, and I would need to change trains twice but as this was classed as a slow route it would only cost around £15 yet it would take about six hours to get to Düsseldorf, without hesitation I bought the ticket and made my way to the platform.

Even though I was told this was a slow and cheap route I didn't expect the train to resemble an old London underground tube train, but that is what pulled into the station. I suppose a cheap ticket was a cheap ticket and once I boarded this train it was obvious that this was no London underground train, it was clean, warm, comfortable, quiet, smooth and didn't smell one bit.

With my bags stowed I was off to pastures new. My first change was at the Dutch city of Roermond I only had five minutes to change to the Venlo train. But when I arrived in Venlo, I had a four hour wait for the connecting train to Düsseldorf the first stop in Germany, it was indeed the long way round.

I pondered over exploring Venlo, but I decided against it as I needed to make sure I was on time and on route for Stuttgart. Venlo train station didn't have as much grandeur as Maastricht, it seemed to be open to the elements and modern looking. The wind tunnelled through the station with very little to slow it down. After finding some platform benches tucked back alongside some drinks vending machines, it seemed I had found adequate cover from the wind and accessible hot beverages. I didn't have money to waste and thanks to Saskia I still had my packed lunch to eat. Which consisted of two soft bread rolls filled with potato salad and some type of sliced meat, it tasted amazing I could taste the care which went into making them. In addition to these rolls, I had a small chocolate bar, a yogurt bar and a small orange everything a growing boy needed.

After sparingly eating my packed lunch and a few cups of vending machine coffee the Düsseldorf train pulled onto the platform, as I stepped onto this train, I could feel the heaters had been on. This train was a modern intercity with reclining seats and lots of leg room, but the best thing about this train was it was barely half full. Once I picked out a quiet corner, I got myself comfortable knowing soon I would be back in Germany and in less than 48hrs since I had my passport stolen, I was halfway to getting help.

Chapter 15
Back in Germany at long last

The train rolled into Düsseldorf at about six in the evening, the platform cleared quite quickly with everyone rushing to their connecting trains or taxis. I was the last person to clear the platform as I needed to decide where to go from here. I seemed to follow the natural flow following people up the stairs along the walkway and down into the main departure hall. I then branched off and joined a que for the ticket office.

Once I got to the ticket assistant, I ask if she spoke English and if she knew the cheapest way to get to Stuttgart. She was extremely helpful, and she told me about a ticket called a "Wochenende Karte" translated to a "weekend card" this ticket was only valid on slow trains not express trains, but you could travel anywhere in Germany all weekend for just 25DM about £15. If I had known about this ticket earlier, I might have found it helpful, but you live and learn. The assistant helped plan my route which involved changing four times to eventually get to Stuttgart at about midday the following day.

My first train of many wasn't due to depart till 22:00HRS so I had just over three hours to kill.

After a short walk around the station, I found a small shop where I stocked up with snacks and supplies to see me through the next 12 hours or, then I returned to the relative warmth and security of the platform to await my first train. After watching the platform clock and the coming and goings of one train after the other eventually it was my turn to board.

The first two changes went seamlessly as I had only minutes to change trains it was a relief to find the train I needed happened to be on the adjoining platforms. So, as I stepped off one train, I only had to take no more than ten steps and I was on my next train. The German transport system worked like clockwork, it seemed the trains were never late and as a passenger you could never afford to be late as you would most definitely miss your train.

When I got to Frankfurt all trains stopped as the station closed for cleaning at 1. 30am. This didn't just mean I could not get on a train, I could not even stay on the platform. Everyone had to vacate the station until it reopened 2 hours later. I made my way to the main entrance to wait with a few other unfortunate souls who had the misfortune of missing their last train home.

I was grateful for a few things, I was grateful for the clement weather, I was grateful for having my backpack to sit on and above all I was grateful that the station was only closed for two hours. Once the station reopened with a fresh scent of cleaning fluids in the air, I made my way across the polished floor to the notice boards to see which platform I needed. Once I was at the platform, I then realised I still had 3 hours to wait but at least I was back in the warmth of the station. After a few hours of fighting against the desire of closing my eyes and falling asleep on the platform bench, I was joined by an elderly lady who was waiting for the same train as she was going to visit her grandson in Stuttgart.

She talked a lot, and she was asking where I was going and when she saw my camping equipment she started reminiscing over when she went camping in her youth in the harz mountain an area famous for its natural beauty and landscapes.

It was nice to hear her stories and then it suddenly dawned on me that this old lady had been speaking to me in German and to my amazement I had been replying in her native tongue without even thinking about it. Up until this point I was not aware of just how much German I had learnt whilst working in the circus. I felt a great feeling of accomplishment at being able to communicate with this kind old soul.

After helping her board, the train to Stuttgart, I got myself comfortable knowing I was on my last leg at last. Once we pulled out of the station it seemed no time at all before I was being awoken by the old lady with a shake and a smile on her face, as she announced that we were pulling into Stuttgart train station.

With bleary eyes from my travels, I said goodbye to the old lady as she made her way up the platform to meet up with her eagerly awaiting grandson.

My attention quickly returned to the reason I was here in the first place to find the British consulate and to get my new passport. On the wall next to the exit was a tourist information map surrounded by a big plastic frame, it had a big arrow pointing at where I was then on the edge there was a list of places like the Theatre, Museums, Market, Cathedral it seemed to have everywhere someone might want to visit. Next to each named place there was a button, when you pressed the button, a light would illuminate on the map to show were it was located. After looking down the list it soon became apparent that the British consulate was not on the list but there was a button for the police station so I decided this might be the best place to start and according to the map it was less than five minutes away.

After a few dead ends and wrong turns, I eventually stumbled across the police station, the information map was ok if you had a photographic memory but that was one thing I did not possess.

After explaining my situation to the officer at the front desk. He grabbed a leaflet which opened to a map of the city and marked on it where I was and then were I needed to be.

To my relief it looked to be only a few miles away. Just as I was thinking my problems were all over, one of the passing officers interrupted and said that the consulate was closed as it was Sunday, but it should open at 09:30 the following morning. While studying the map I was given, I noticed there was a big city park not far from the station so I asked the officer if I could sleep in the park just for one night. The officer said I could but in the same breath he said to be careful as there is a lot of dangerous people about the park at night.

With those words of caution and my portable map, I made my way to the city park to set up camp.

The city park consisted of winding footpaths bordered with mature trees and benches. There were also wide-open stretches of grassed areas, on the face of it, it looked like the ideal place to camp. As the sun was starting to set, I noticed a distinct change, all the benches started to become occupied by the homeless, vagrants and unfortunate citizens of the city. I seemed to be surrounded by the areas of society hidden, unnoticed and unseen in the light of day.

With the daylight fading quickly I found a secluded area to pitch my tent, I was on the edge of a grassed area with a thick hedge row partially encircling my tent at the top of a slope, so I had a good vantage point over the park, away from the main footpaths.

 I made myself comfortable and within half an hour of setting up camp darkness fell, like a blanket all around me which left me feeling lonely and isolated from the world. It took me a while, but I eventually drifted off to sleep.

In what only seemed minutes I was awoken by a bright blinding light followed by footsteps outside my tent. Then a voice said in German, "police! come out with your hands up!" I froze for a second then replied, "OK I'm coming". Has I unzipped the tent and crawled out, I was faced with two police officers stood there with their pistols drawn and pointing at me.

I raised my hands to show I was not a threat and said in a startled manor "hello officers do you speak English".
With the officers happy that I was not a threat to them they lowered their weapons, and I was relieved to find that one of them could speak quite good English.
After I had regained my composure of the situation the officer asked why I was there. I explained that the officer at the police station said I could sleep here overnight until the consulate opened.

Then the officer explained that his colleague at the station would have meant I could sleep on a bench or in my sleeping bag, but he wouldn't have advised me to sleep in a tent as it may bring unwanted attention to me.

I was a bit confused as I wasn't doing anything wrong, and I was more comfortable in my tent. The officer went onto explain that two weeks ago a Dutch man set up camp just like me and the police found him dead in his tent the next morning. This man was found murdered he had been stabbed several times and robbed and they were still looking for his attacker.

The police officers said all they could do was advise me not to camp here, they couldn't make me move on, so the choice was mine. Once I had weighed up my options. I decided to stay put I knew it would attract more attention if I was to start taking my tent down in the dark.

But I also decided to upgrade my security just in case, so once the police had moved on. I got my head torch and retrieved my fishing kit which was stowed in the handle of my survival knife and spent the next 20 minutes setting a trip wire with my fishing line around my tent so at least I would be forewarned if someone was coming to get me.

Then I laid there on top of my sleeping bag with my knife next to me for the rest of the night. Unsurprisingly as my senses were on high alert not a sound came from my tent, at times I thought I might have been breathing too loud. I didn't get much if any sleep that night.

As soon as the morning sun broke, a feeling of relief came over me as I had survived the night with only my pride being hurt, knowing in hindsight that I could have slept all night without being worried about the murderer coming knocking. Exhausted I gathered my things and made my way out of the park to get to the British Consulate for when the offices opened and to hopefully make my way home.

In my head I had a picture of what I thought a British Consulate would look like. I thought it would be a grand old looking building adorned with the flags of Great Britain and have big Metal gates, and of course with armed guards posted at the entrance holding Heckler & Koch MP5 submachine guns.

I was very much mistaken as I turned the corner to see the reality of what a British Consulate looked like. The building looked quite subdued like any block of offices you might find in any town centre. It resembled a tax office or job centre more than a British Consulate, if it hadn't had a sign next to the door, I might have walked straight past.

On the ground floor I was somewhat relieved that they had a security guard with a metal detector wand. Then I realised that I had my personal protection equipment on me, my nun chucks were taken off me as the guard said they only had one purpose and that was to be used as a weapon.

To my surprise he didn't have the same opinion about my six-inch survival knife, he wouldn't allow me to take the knife in with me, but he was prepared to give me it back when I left as the knife had a legitimate use. A small price to pay I thought.
I was directed to sit outside an office on the first floor and I was told to wait for an advisor to call me in. After only minutes a young lady called my name.

She must have been in her early 20s about my age. She had long dark hair platted all the way down her back, you might say she had been at the front of the que when they were handing out good looks, she was extremely beautiful, I was to find she also had the brains to match.

I explained my predicament and asked if she could help me get a replacement passport. She explained that I would need to prove my identity first and answer some questions like were my passport had been stolen. Then a statement could be taken, and a decision could be made based on the findings of an investigation. So, the interrogation began.

The first of many questions was "how can you prove your identity?" after racking my brain for a while I could only come up with" you can phone my parents in the UK". The lady asked if I had ever been arrested, served time in prison, been fingerprinted or had anything to do with the British armed forces.

Once I told her about my time in the Army, she seemed to be happy that she could obtain the information she required, without having to talk to my mother or farther. Which was a relief to both of us.

The lady asked where I had my passport stolen, so I grabbed my road atlas and pointed at the area of Belgium where I was robbed. She looked at me with a confused expression on her face and asked why had I come to Stuttgart to report the missing passport as there was much closer British Consulates located in Paris or Brussels from where I was robbed?

I explained my reasoning and that I was not aware of the closer Consulate, and of course that the Dutch police had said this was the only Consulate which could issue me with a replacement passport.

With a smile and a cheeky chuckle, she said "the Dutch police were right, this is the only Consulate in Europe that can issue a passport, but they had failed to tell you that we can post them to any other British Consulate in Europe or indeed the world".

This was the first time she had someone travel over 400 miles past at least three other British Consulate to come direct to her office and she found this quite amusing, even I had to see the funny side.

Once this lady had written up her statement and checked with the British Ministry of Defence that I was who I said I was she was more than happy to request a temporary 3-month replacement passport.

In addition to this she authorised a rail warrant to allow me to travel by train to a ferry port of my choice. As I had my road atlas on my lap, I chose the first port I saw that went to the UK. The port of Zeebrugge in Belgium which would take me on to Hull in the North of England which would leave me about 100 miles from home. I had everything mapped out once I had my train tickets, I should be back in England within 48 hrs, back and broke in England, to start a job in the factory I didn't want and to pay back my Dad for the £100 he had lent me. But for the experiences I had, to me, it was all worthwhile.

Even though I would have preferred to have returned with money in my pocket and a smile on my face, life doesn't always turn out the way you first expect. I thanked the staff at the Consulate and collected my knife from the security desk then made my way to the train station to begin my last leg home.

I was relieved to find that the rail warrant entitled me to travel on the direct express trains and intercity trains unlike the slow trains I had to suffer to get to Stuttgart.

It was still to be three train changes, my first change was Koln then onto Brussels, Brugge and finally arriving in Zeebrugge some eight and a half hours later. The biggest change I found with the direct routes was the comfort which came with this. After the tiresome journey to Stuttgart, combined with the lack of sleep in the city park I grabbed as much sleep as I could on this broken journey homeward. I only managed light sleep as I was interrupted frequently, any indication of the train slowing down woke me, be it the sound of the engine, breaks or just movement around me.

I imagine this was because I was worried that I might miss my connecting trains, if I were to oversleep. I wouldn't say I was totally recharged when I stepped off the train in Zeebrugge, but I was relieved as I could smell the sea air, and everything seemed to be going to plan for once. As soon as I was out of the station, I asked a taxi driver how far it was to the ferry port I was told it would be about 15 minutes by taxi or a 40 minutes' walk.

The taxi would have cost me around £10 so I opted for the 40-minute free walk, if anything it stretched my legs after being sat for quite some time.
It must have been close to 8 O'clock in the evening when I arrived at the port and I could see in the distance that a ferry was coming into dock, just in time I thought.
I made my way to the ticket office with my new passport in hand, and a smile on my face. I asked if I could have a one-way ticket to Hull. The ticket officer asked, "how many would be traveling sir". Just me I replied, I'm traveling on my own.

With that the officer paused then went on to explain to me that, as the crossing was overnight everyone would need to book a cabin and I would need to pay a single supplement on top of my normal ticket price.

When I asked how much that would be in English pounds, he got out his calculator and after tapping the buttons for a while he replied "75 pound sterling sir for the cheapest cabin available". This was out of my budget.

The officer advised me to try one of the other ports Ostend, Rotterdam or Dunkerque as all these ports offered shorter crossings at a fraction of the cost.

 Knowing I wouldn't be getting a ferry from here I made my way to the road heading out of the port and started hitchhiking once more. I was hoping the cars coming off the ferry would be going in the direction of any of these other ports.
With the constant stream of traffic, I was thinking that I had a good chance of someone stopping. Most of the vehicles were English, all I needed was a bit of that elusive luck.

Car after car passed me, some small some big, some towing caravans, the one thing they all had in common was they were all driving past. Then a line of bigger vehicles thundered past trucks and vans of every size followed by a sudden silence as the ferry seemed to be empty once more.

Chapter 16
The Hippy

Not knowing where to head for from here, I threw my backpack down at the base of a streetlight and started to assess the road atlas once more. Just as I was thinking of giving in and making camp for the night, I heard a spluttery engine sound coming from the direction of the ferry. As I turned, I saw this dark green high topped long wheelbase van with sidecar racing team written across the bonnet coming towards me. I walked back to the roadside and raised my thumb hoping this would be the last lift I would need.

To my relief the van stopped, and I was faced with a long-haired man who resembled a peace-loving hippy in many ways, from his round spectacles and his small goatee beard down to the first words he spoke being "Hay Man, are you going my way man" in a slight Black country accent. I grabbed my bag and made myself comfortable next to this friendly free spirit.

This man asked me where I was heading and to his surprise, I said "any port what can take me back to the UK". He asked me why I wanted to go home when there was nothing special in the UK to go back for. It was like he had turned into a travel agent wanting to sell me the holiday of a lifetime, his excitement would have been infectious if it wasn't for how physically and emotionally drained, I felt. I explained that I had been travelling around Europe for quite some time and I had hit a run of bad luck regarding finding work of late.

I also explained that I must return to England as I had borrowed some money off my father so I could get a replacement temporary passport and I would need to pay him back, so I had run out of options, and I had to go home.

Hearing this the hippy pulled the van off the road and said, "do you fancy a brew man everything seems better after a cup of tea". With that he stood up and opened a curtain which was hanging behind our seats to reveal a fully functional kitchen and much more.

From the outside this van looked like a normal long wheelbase high-top van, with "side car race team" written on the front and side panels. But once you stepped into the back it was much more than a van. At the back doors there were two levels on the top level there was a full king size bed under this on the lower level was a full-size single bed on one side and a fully functioning shower room on the other.

Every inch of space seemed to be utilised. In the middle of the van was a seating area with comfortable seating and a television, then backing onto the front seats was the kitchen area. This was indeed the best stealth motor home I had ever seen.

As we were drinking our cups of tea the conversation flowed, it became apparent that my host was called Richard, and he came from a place called Sandwell near Dudley. He had planned to make this trip with a friend, who had pulled out at the last minute. But nevertheless, Richard still set off.

Richard and his absent friend had arranged some work before leaving the UK, something I would have benefited from doing myself in hindsight.

His first place of work was to be a Marquee hire company in Belgium called Neptunus and he had two days to get there, which was plenty of time.

After sitting through the sales pitch of a lifetime Richard asked if I would like to take his friends place as the Marquee company was expecting two English men not one and to top it off the money was good. We would be a part of the traveling team erecting Marquee's all over Belgum and France. Accommodation was also provided by the company, and it wasn't in a circus caravan, they put everyone up in bed and breakfasts or hotels in the areas we were to travel to. Just the thought of earning some good money and sleeping in a clean bed before going back to the UK, was enough for me to take Richard up on his most generous offer.

After we had finished our informative chat and cups of tea, we made our way to a parking up area to wind down as we had time on our side. Richard disappeared onto his top bunk then suddenly reemerged holding a bottle of red wine and I small wooden box.

He told me to grab two glasses from the kitchen cupboard, by the time I turned round he had opened his small wooden box, and he was in the prosses of making the neatest six inch roll up I had ever seen. As soon as I saw this man, I knew he must have been a smoker, of the herbal variety, a true hippy of course.

Once we had finished the bottle and a few herbal smokes, I made my excuses and dragged myself into the single bunk to drift off into a dream like state, feeling totally relaxed and safe for the first time in a long time.

The following morning, I was gently awoken by the swaying of the van, as I opened my eyes, I could see the road ahead through a small gap in the curtain.

As I stretched my legs and gave out a big morning yawn. Richard called back "your awake then!" he didn't want to disturb me, so he had set off to get to the Office of the Marquee company early, he said he thought it might look good if we got there a day early. But in the back of my mind, I thought he might have set off earlier to give me less time to change my mind. Nevertheless, I was on my way to a new job from the water's edge once more but this time I was travelling in comfort and relative style than what I had become accustomed too. After making us both a cup of tea and a slice of toast I took my place beside my travelling companion and soon to be work mate Richard.

It seemed to be no time at all when we pulled up to the office of the marquee company. I had in my mind that the marquees would be for small country fairs, wedding and such like.

Even though this was part of the services the company offered, they had a more corporate section to the company, and this is where the big Marquees were used for music concerts, art displays and very opulent events indeed.

These marquees could be up to 40 meters wide and if you wanted a long marquee, they would just add on an extra section, some of them looked more like aircraft hangars than marquees. I started to realise why they paid such good money.

Once we had filled in the relevant paperwork, we were asked to open a Belgian bank account, so they could pay in our monthly wages. If we needed money to help us through till our first payday, they could give us an advance on our wages of 10,000 Belgium francs once we had worked a week which seemed fair.

We found a bank called ING and deposited the minimum amount of 1000 Belgium francs to open an account. This seemed like a lot of money but as the exchange rate was around 53 Belgian francs to the pound, in reality it only cost £20, which to my relief was within my limited budget. We left holding our bank books which allowed us to deposit and withdraw funds across Europe.

Once we started, we were working with a team of about 10 men, it was like trying to fit into a well-oiled machine knowing very little of what was needed to be done. Me and Richard just muddled through the first few days. Very few people spoke English so we followed then copied and picked up the job as we went along. Once we got to grips with how the marquees went together the job became a lot easier and in no time, we were up to speed and more accepted by our colleagues.

At the end of each day, we were all bundled into a minibus and taken to our accommodation which was normally a budget hotel, which was to me the height of luxury. A hot shower at the end of each day was a long way from washing myself down out of a metal bucket which I had to endured in the circus. This coupled with a nice evening meal followed by an all you can eat breakfast the following morning really did set us up for the day's work. We worked Monday to Friday and at the weekends we were back into the comfort of the stealth camper.

On the first weekend off Richard needed to take a trip over the boarder to Holland to top up on his marijuana supplies, he was aware that not everyone was accepting of the smoking of Cannabis, so he tried to keep work and down time separate. At the end of each week, we would drive out of the area before parking up for the weekend and commence smoking and drinking and we even grabbed the chance to do a bit of fishing. Down time was truly down time.

Pay day couldn't come quick enough as our funds were dwindling, and work seemed to be going well. On the Friday of our third week, I was working on laying the floor panels with a 3-man team and Richard was working with a team putting the side panels into place, while they were waiting for more panels, they all went for a cigarette break. Unfortunately for Richard while he was making a roll up, a small piece of marijuana he hadn't notice in his tobacco pouch found its way into his roll up and as soon as he lit up everyone around him could smell the distinctive smell.

Nobody said a word, but the first thing Richard was asked to do when he turned up for work Monday morning was a drug test. Richard refused to take the test and handed in his work gear, which also meant that I could not work there either as I was dependant on Richard's hospitality.

After a very quiet walk back to the van with Richard we made our way a few miles up the road to decide what to do next. Richard couldn't apologise enough but I told him not to worry about it, I would have had to quit at some point as I still only had a temporary passport.

 After another night of drinking red wine and smoking the odd joint, I agreed to go to the office to ask when we would receive our first and last wage. The boss explained to me that they couldn't pay us early, but he assured me that we would both be paid all the money we were owed at the end of the month into our accounts.

I think he was just as upset to lose us as we were to be going, but his hands were tied. I believed he would pay us without a doubt. So, I returned to Richard to break the good news we only had to wait a week till the end of the month. After a few days relaxing Richard decided that he wanted to head off to the French boarder to wait for his pay, then move into France to do some fruit picking. As I still had to get home, we parted company giving me three days under canvas, until payday. To make things easier for me, Richard dropped me about 10 miles away from the port of Ostend so once my money appeared I could get straight across to Ramsgate and then home. I calculated that I was owed around £1000 for the three weeks I had worked which was more than the circus had paid me in total, so I would have plenty to get myself home, pay my dad back and have funds left for my next adventure.

I had a bit of food and drink to last me the three days, that's if I rationed out my remaining supplies sparingly. Sure, I wouldn't be eating like a king but at least I would be eating something, to me it was just a waiting game.

Chapter 17
The Waiting Game

As I had decided to sit out my three days under canvas, I looked for a secluded area to make camp not wanting to be disturbed by passersby. I noticed on the outskirts a small hillock with a small piece of woodland situated on the top, this seemed to be a good vantage point and the fields directly under the woodland looked like they were grain fields with a long wheat like crops growing in them. I thought this could give me adequate cover from prying eyes, so I started the climb.

Once I had got to the hedge line with the grain on one side and the woodland on the other, I could see that I had picked the perfect spot, it was secluded, and I could see the lights of Ostend over the grain when I stood up. I carefully cleared an area of the hedge row with the woodland behind me not wanting to damage or disturb the farmer's crop just in case I was found.

After clearing enough space for my tent, I grabbed my rolled-up ground sheet and started to unroll it. As I opened the ground sheet all I could smell was the musty eye watering smell of mould followed by the realisation that I had committed one of the cardinal sins when packing a tent. I had packed it wet and not aired it out in good time, I had not aired it out at all, so it had been festering under the single bed of the stealth camper undisturbed for nearly four weeks.

As I tried to separate the mould infested flysheet from the ground sheet, I was covered by a sudden release of mould spores as a gust of wind blew across the hedge line. With my eyes and lips tightly shut I turned my back and moved upwind of the tent so not to inhale any of the toxic spores and rethink my plan from here.

Once the wind had calmed, I had a plan! I wrapped my scarf around my face to stop the spores from entering my lungs, then I started cutting the fly sheet away from the waterproof ground sheet with my knife.

Once I had gathered all the mould covered fly sheet, I started to clean and air out the waterproof outer covering of the tent and ground sheet with what little water I could spare out of my supplies. After an hour of modifying my small ridge tent I was left with a ground sheet the poles and the outer waterproof cover, so once I had erected the outer cover and pegged in the guide ropes, I was left with an open-ended shelter with a loose fitted ground sheet and a lot of ventilation. I organised my things to weigh down the ground sheet and rolled out my sleeping bag, I would say I had managed to get myself quite comfortable against all odds. I was just relieved it wasn't winter as I would have been in trouble if it were. So, with a lesson learnt I settled down for my first night in my temporary shelter.

Most of the three days were plagued with yes, more rain! At times I had a small stream of water passing the front of my tent, it seemed the grain was getting a good watering as was I.

I managed to refill my water bottle by catching some redirected rain by placing my bottle under a knot I had tied on my guide rope which at the height of the downpours had a constant stream of water drizzling off it. To my relief the water stayed out of the main sleeping area under my tent and very little water migrated on to my belongings.

To my surprise I went unnoticed for the full three days. Time seemed to fly, I spent the daylight hours writing in my travel journal, sorting through my equipment while trying to keep my things away from any unwanted drips.

I even managed to stitch up my thread bared socks so they could last me that little bit longer. With all my batteries dead in all my torches, my bedtime was dictated by when the sun was to set. I went for a few walks whenever the rain stopped just to break up the monotony and stretch my legs. I was so excited to wake up on payday, not only because I had finished the last of my supplies the night before but also it was the day I was to go home.

At the break of day I quickly packed my tent not caring it was wet as I had already decided that it was going in the first bin I was to come across.

I was on a mission to get to the nearest bank and then the ferry port.

I had planned the route I was to take; I could see the outskirts of Ostend from where I had been sleeping and according to my map the nearest built-up area was the region of Stene-Dorp, which would be classed as part of the suburbs of Ostend. Based on the information in my road atlas there was shops, petrol stations, restaurants and even an odd church or two so I was hoping that this area would also have a branch of the ING bank. With the clouds clearing for a seemingly good day and my belongings on my back I headed for Stene-Dorp to pick up my last earnings from Europe.

Chapter 18
Payday!

As I walked through the Stene-Dorp Area I deposited the remains of my trusty tent into a bin then I started to follow the flow of working people heading towards the shops and market area. The shutters were being lifted and the shop keepers were just starting to set out their wares and one by one the shops opened to welcome in the first customers of the day. I could smell, on the breeze, mouthwatering aromas coming from the nearby cafes and bakeries, but I would have to wait for the banks to open before I could taste these culinary delights. It took a while before I found the bank but unfortunately the bank was not to open for a few hours, so I walked on past and found a bench outside a church right next to a small bakery to wait.

The weather was clear for the first time in quite a while and I could feel the sun's rays heating up my back as I sat there and watched the people going about their business, I felt invisible to all, time seemed to slow down, but I got a gentle reminder every half an hour from the church clocks chimes.

At long last, it was time I moved on. With time to spare and a spring in my step I made my way towards the bank to make sure I was to be first in the queue. While passing the bakeries and coffee shops, I found myself making a mental list of what confectionery I was to buy once I had my money.

I stood outside the big looming wooden doors of the bank relieved to hear the many bolts and locks being released, as the bank clerks were ready for business. With a smile and a wink, I stepped into the bank and up to the first cashier's booth with my passport and bank book tightly grasped in my hand as I was thinking there was nothing better than pay day.

I handed over my bank book and passport and told the cashier that I would like to withdraw my wages please, with a few taps on his keyboard he said that no funds had been deposited.

I asked him to check again as my wage should be in today, so he did, but to my disbelief the cashier came back to me with the same response. He went on to say that the wages might be in later but now there was nothing in my account except for my initial deposit I had made to open the account a month ago.

I thanked the cashier for his time and told him I would try later. I stood outside the bank not sure what to do, my body was starting to show signs of weakness, due to not eating much at all over the previous 3 days, yet I still had time to wait. Not wanting to expel any more energy than necessary, I made my way back to the bench by the church once more. I had been told some time ago that churches always have an outside tap so anyone could get access to water 24 hours a day if they needed it.

With time on my hands, I looked around the church and to my surprise I found a tap. Without delay I filled my water bottle so at least I had the benefit of clean cold water, still not the cakes and pastries that my mind had told my stomach I was soon to have.

The clouds seemed to be gathering once more but I was grateful that the rain held off.
As I sat there still feeling invisible to all around, I kept myself at one end of the bench so if anyone needed to sit for a while they could.

 I'm not sure if it was the clouds overhead which stopped people sitting on the bench or me sat there looking slightly dishevelled and worse for wear. But everyone was just going about their business and they didn't even seem to talk to one another, they didn't seem to be a very sociable bunch in Ostend. After a few hours sat there I made my way back to the bank at midday and unfortunately again at 4 O' clock just before they shut.

To be told yet again that the money hadn't been deposited.

I felt disheartened with this news, and I started to question if I had the right day or if I had understood what the boss had told me regarding my pay, while I made my way back to the church bench once more.

I found my mind starting to recall the conversation I had with the boss, in minute detail. I could see his facial expressions and hear what he had told me, that he would ensure the money would be paid and that I had his word. But with his word or not, I was facing a night sat on a bench having not eaten a proper meal for nearly four days.

I was hoping that once the bank reopened the following morning my money would be there.

As the shops started to shut for the night all around me, I tried to make myself as comfortable as I could for the long night ahead. By 8 O'clock the streets had cleared, the area was silent and shut down, it seemed my body was doing the same. I started to feel pain like I had never felt before, it felt like my stomach was eating itself.

When I moved, I felt pain in every muscle like they were on strike refusing to work without moaning about it. My eyes were hurting, my head was pounding, it was obvious to me I had to seek medical attention immediately. I remembered that I had seen a signpost for a hospital on the way to the bank so I forced myself to move while I still could. I got to a crossroads where I had seen the sign for the hospital and their underneath was an arrow indicating the direction and distance of 1 kilometre.

This was to be the hardest kilometre I had ever walk, with every step accompanied with pain followed by nausea. I walked past a fast-food van selling burgers to people coming out of nearby pubs, the smell just seemed to make my symptoms worsen.
 The hospital was situated just outside the built-up area, and I could see from a distance a helicopter landing on its roof taking a poor unfortunate soul for life saving treatment.

As I approached the automatic doors, I couldn't see any staff or the rushing about of people you would expect at a hospital in the UK, in fact I couldn't see a soul. When I got to the doors, they didn't open then I saw an intercom box with an arrow pointing at a button. With my head resting on the glass, I pressed the button and said, "I need to see a doctor".

To my surprise a faint voice came back in English "sorry we are closed ".

I explained again that I needed a doctor and the voice explained that they only accepted admissions by ambulance or helicopter at night, then he advised me to call an ambulance if I thought it, was an emergency.

This dumfounded me and left me speechless, but one thing was obvious I was not going to get any help here. So, with a deep breath in, I turned to make my way back towards the bench, not knowing what to do or even if I could make it back.

As I got back to where the burger van was the front serving hatch was down and it looked like he was just packing up for the night, out of desperation I approached the side door and asked, "have you any food", followed by "I have no money". This man just looked at me with a blank expression on his face as it was clear that he didn't understand a word of English. I glanced over this man's shoulder and saw some cooked items in the display cabinet, so I pointed at these items and said "food" then I pointed at my pockets and turned them inside out to show him I had no money. With this a smile came over his bemused face as he turned and picked up a cardboard tray and piled as much of the leftovers as he could.

I felt conflicting emotions, I was grateful, embarrassed, sad and happy all at the same time as he passed me this tray of food, tears started rolling down my cheeks.

I had never been in the position that I had to beg for anything, I took pride in paying my way in life, yet I found myself in this position taking charity off a stranger and having to beg for food.

I thanked this man and made my way to a nearby bench with tears still rolling down my face from the kindness this stranger had shown me. I started to eat this warm mix of Belgium fast food. In the tray were two long thin sausages and two large balls of meat, as soon as the food touched my tongue it was like fireworks were going off in my mouth.

Instantly all my aches and pains seemed to vanish, as my energy levels lifted, I felt totally recharged in seconds. It wasn't until some months later I found out that I was suffering from salt deficiency one of the first signs of starvation, a feeling I never wanted to experience ever again. Once I had finished this much needed nutrition, I made my way back to the church bench to wait for the sun to rise on hopefully my last day without money.

As the usual hustle and bustle started all around me, I made my way back to the Bank hoping with all my heart that this torment would be over at long last. Within no time at all I was stood in front of the bank clerk once again, eagerly awaiting his response once he tapped the account details into his keyboard.

To my disbelief he asked me "how would you like your money" with a smile on his face. After I got over the shock, I asked how much was in my account, so he printed out a balance and it read 46,780 Belgium France which was just over £1000. Without hesitation I asked for it all in hundreds and if he could then close the account which he did.

I walked out of the Bank feeling like I was on cloud nine, it was like my rucksack was full of air as I ran back to the bakery next to the bench, I had spent so much time on.

I must have past many cafés and shops to get there but this was the bakery I knew and had smelt the most over the past days and this is where I wanted to spend just a little of my money. When I got to the doorway I wasn't even out of breath, I approached the counter to be faced with a young female shop assistant then I started placing my order by pointing at everything I had desired for quite some time.

To my surprise the assistant didn't move, she just stepped back and looked over to the manager and said something in her native tongue. I immediately assumed she must have thought I had no money, so I pulled out of my pocket a hand full of banknotes and said, "I have money". It seems I hadn't gone unnoticed while I took up occupancy on the bench outside after all.

With a nod from the manager the shop assistance started to fill paper bags with the delights I had yearned for.

While she was adding up the cost, I noticed behind her head a figure in the mirror and the figure I was looking at, was me! I had not seen myself for some time and I looked like a tramp with dirty smelly clothes, my skin looked to have ground in dirt compressed in every pore, all this with a substantial unkept beard. I felt so ashamed I could hardly recognise myself. I gave the young lady the money for the goods and a healthy tip to apologise in some way for my appearance, then I made my way back into the street. After devouring these delights and nearly making myself sick in the process I continued down the street and found a shop to buy a bar of soap, deodorant and a razor.

Further along the street I found a laundrette. After putting aside, the cleanest clothes I could find in my backpack I emptied the rest of my well-worn belongings into the washing machine to start cleaning the grime of the past days away. I had noticed some public toilet across the road, so while my things were washing, I made my way into the disabled toilets to start my makeover, to get me back to feeling human once more.

I stripped off in front of the hand basin and gave myself a strip wash and shave, before I put on the clothes I had taken from my bag. As I washed soap off my face after having a shave, I looked in the polished stainless-steel mirror to see I was back. I walked out of that toilet feeling normal at long last. I found a shop to buy a new rucksack then I returned to the laundrette to place my clothes into the dryer and transfer all my equipment over into the comfiest backpack I had ever owned. When I walked out of that laundrette I looked and felt like a completely different person to whom walked in.

While I walked around Ostend, I bought myself a brand-new jacket then made my way to the Ostend ferry port to buy my ticket at long last. Everything seemed to be going to plan without any unforeseen problems this time.

Before I knew it, I was on the top deck of the ferry overlooking the harbour, with money in my pocket and a feeling of relief and some sense of accomplishment. Thoughts flashed through my mind of the people I had helped, and the people who had helped me when I really needed it, also the friendships I had forged regardless of any language barriers and all the good and bad situations I had found myself in.

As the ferry set sale to take me home, I felt content that I had truly experienced what being human really was, the good parts and the bad and I was looking forward to my next adventure.

The End, or the start of my next adventure!